MARIA THERESA

AND

THE HOUSE OF AUSTRIA

Men and Their Times

VOLUMES PUBLISHED OR IN PREPARATION

The Use of History, by A. L. Rowse
Pericles and Athens, by A. R. Burn
Alexander the Great and the Hellenistic World, by A. R. Burn
Cicero and the Roman Republic, by W. K. Lacey
Julius Caesar and Rome, by J. P. D. Balsdon
Agricola and Roman Britain, by A. R. Burn
Constantine and the Conversion of Europe, by A. H. M. Jones
William I and the Norman Conquest, by F. Barlow
John Wycliffe and the Beginnings of English Nonconformity, by K. B. McFarlane
Henry V and the Invasion of France, by E. F. Jacob
Ivan III and the Unification of Russia, by Ian Grey
Lorenzo dei Medici and Renaissance Italy, by C. M. Ady
Machiavelli and Renaissance Italy, by John Hale
Erasmus and the Northern Renaissance, by Margaret Mann Phillips
Martin Luther and the Reformation, by A. G. Dickens
Henry VIII and the English Reformation, by J. K. McConica
Thomas Cromwell and the English Reformation, by A. G. Dickens
Cranmer and the English Reformation, by F. E. Hutchinson
Elizabeth I and the Unity of England, by J. Hurstfield
William the Silent and Dutch Independence, by C. H. Wilson
Raleigh and the British Empire, by D. B. Quinn
Richelieu and the French Monarchy, by C. V. Wedgwood
Oliver Cromwell and the Puritan Revolution, by Maurice Ashley
Louis XIV and the Greatness of France, by Maurice Ashley
Peter the Great and the Emergence of Russia, by B. H. Summer
Chatham and the British Empire, by Sir Charles Grant Robertson
Catherine the Great and the Expansion of Russia, by Gladys Scott Thomson
Frederick the Great and the Rise of Prussia, by D. B. Horn
Benjamin Franklin and the American People, by Esmond Wright
Warren Hastings and British India, by Sir Penderel Moon
Washington and the American Revolution, by Esmond Wright
Robespierre and the French Revolution, by J. M. Thompson
Napoleon and the Awakening of Europe, by Felix Markham
Thomas Jefferson and American Democracy, by Max Beloff
Marx, Proudhon and European Socialism, by J. Hampden Jackson
Abraham Lincoln and the United States, by K. C. Wheare
Napoleon III and the Second Empire, by J. P. T. Bury
Bismarck and Modern Germany, by W. N. Medlicott
Alexander II and the Modernisation of Russia, by W. E. Mosse
Gladstone and Liberalism, by J. L. Hammond and M. R. D. Foot
Livingstone and Africa, by Jack Simmons
Clemenceau and the Third Republic, by J. Hampden Jackson
Lenin and the Russian Revolution, by Christopher Hill
Stalin and Soviet Russia, by G. F. Hudson
Gandhi and Modern India, by Sir Penderel Moon
Roosevelt and Modern America, by J. A. Woods

MARIA THERESA

and

The House of Austria

C. A. MACARTNEY

LAWRENCE VERRY INC.
MYSTIC, CONN.

SBN 340 05253 8
Copyright © 1969 C. A. Macartney

Printed and bound in Great Britain

Introduction to the Series

This series has been undertaken in the conviction that no subject is more important than history. For though the conquests of natural science (nuclear fission, the exploration of space, genetic advance, bacteriology, etc.) have given their character to the age, it is actually a greater need to gain control of the forces of nature loosed upon us. The prime urgency, the deepest necessity is in the human field: to understand the nature and condition of man as a pre-condition of better controls, and fewer disasters, in the world of politics and society.

There is no better introduction to this sphere, and the understanding of its problems, than history. *Some* knowledge of history, we feel, ought to prevent some mistakes: at every point we can learn vicariously from the experience of others before us.

To take one point only – the understanding of politics: how can we understand the world of affairs around us, if we do not know how it came to be what it is? How to interpret the United States, or Soviet Russia, France, Germany or Britain without some knowledge of their history?

Some evidence of the growing awareness of this may be seen in the great increase of interest in history among the general public, and in the much larger place the subject has come to take in education.

The most congenial, as well as the most concrete and practical, approach to history is the biographical: through the lives of great men whose careers have been significant in history. Fashions in historical writing have their ups and downs; men's and women's lives have their

perennial interest – though in this series we are chiefly concerned to show their historical significance, the contribution they made to their age: *Men and their Times*.

A generation ago historical biographies were rather unfashionable with analytical historians and technicians, like Namier: he ended by writing scores of miniature biographies of M.P.s. The detailed analysis of Civil War and Commonwealth has ended by showing that there were almost as many party-divisions as there were individuals. We are back in the realm of biography and the biographical approach to history, since there is no greater diversity, variety and subtlety than in the lives of individual men and women, particularly those who left a mark on their time.

A. L. Rowse

Oxford

Contents

PART ONE

HEIRESS AND BRIDE
1717–1740

I

Maria Theresia (so she was christened) was born in Vienna on May 13, 1717, the second issue of the marriage between Charles of Habsburg, sixth Holy Roman Emperor of the name, and Elisabeth Christine, of the Ducal House of Brunswick-Wolfensbeutel. Hers was thus the most august parentage in Europe, and hers too would be —if hers it became indeed—its stateliest heritage. For her father was not only Emperor by election, as his forbears had been for three centuries before him, but also lord in his own right of vast territories. He had been the younger of his father's two sons, but on the death in 1711 of his elder brother, Joseph, without male heirs, had succeeded to the whole heritage of the 'Austrian' branch of his family: its old nucleus of the Austrias, Styria, Carinthia, Carniola, Gorizia and the Tirol, a complex covering nearly the whole Eastern Alps and their foothills down to Trieste, with outliers further west, together with the Lands of the Bohemian and Hungarian Crowns, acquired in 1526.

While Joseph still lived, Charles had been a claimant to the throne of Spain, rendered vacant in 1700 by the death of the last of the Spanish line of the Habsburgs, and he had spent 7 years of his young manhood in the Peninsula, in pursuit of that dignity, returning to settle in

Vienna only in 1713. The end of the War of the Spanish Succession had forced him to renounce this hope, but had left him with a substantial share of his cousin's heritage: the Spanish Netherlands, Milan, Naples and Sardinia (then exchanged for Sicily). While Maria Theresa was growing up, he lost Naples and Sicily, but his armies, then still led by the great Eugene of Savoy, had, after driving the Turks out of that fringe of Southern Hungary over which Habsburg rule had not thitherto been effective, penetrated into the Balkans and added northern Serbia and western Wallachia to the dominions of the House of Austria.

When Maria Theresa was born it was, indeed, only a possibility that she would succeed to all this; not even a strong probability, far less a certainty. Joseph and Charles had been the last male representatives of their line, and Joseph's death had left Charles the only bearer of the name, except his two nieces, Joseph's daughters. In 1713 he had enacted a family law, the so-called 'Pragmatic Sanction', declaring his will that on his death his entire heritage was to pass, undivided in primogeniture, to his male issue, if any, but failing such, to his female issue: Joseph's daughters, or their issue, were to succeed only if the Carolean line became totally extinct. Since Charles' and Elisabeth's first child, although a boy, had lived only a few months, Maria Theresa, as the next-born, was her father's heiress-presumptive, but even should no later-born brother oust her, her succession, at any rate to the complete heritage, was by no means fully assured. So far as his own subjects were concerned, Charles assured it: none of the dominions which he had inherited was constitutionally entitled to query his will, except Hungary, which up to that date was still only bound to accept the male succession, and in 1722/3 Hungary, too, agreed to accept the female line. But foreign courts were not obliged to accept Charles' *ipse dixit*, the validity of which was, moreover, really questionable: an earlier 'Pact of Mutual Succession', enacted by Charles' father, Leopold, to which Charles himself had expressly assented, had laid down that should both Joseph and Charles die without male issue, Joseph's daughters should take precedence of Charles'. It was also possible, given the tangle of European dynastic genealogies, that some other claimant might dispute the title of Charles' daughter to one or another province.

The quest for guarantees, or at least recognition, of the Pragmatic Sanction was one of Charles' main pre-occupations throughout his reign. Old Prince Eugene said robustly that a strong army and a full purse were the best guarantees, but Charles, who possessed neither of these things, perforce tried the road of diplomacy. He secured the guarantees of Spain in 1725, Russia in 1726, and Britain (and Hanover) and the Netherlands in 1731, that of Hanover through the adoption of a Resolution in favour of an Imperial guarantee, which became Imperial Law on February 3, 1732 (largely owing to the strong advocacy of it by King Frederick William of Prussia). In March 1733 the Elector of Saxony recognised the Sanction *qua* aspirant to the throne of Poland, as did France in September 1735. Meanwhile, when arranging the marriages of Joseph's two daughters, who were his wards, into the ruling houses of Saxony and Bavaria respectively, Charles had made both them and their husbands renounce any claims under the Pact of Mutual Succession.

The assurances were thus fairly numerous, but there were still gaps. The Elector of Bavaria refused to renounce a claim based on his reading of the will of Ferdinand I (d. 1564) which, he maintained, made the Wittelsbachs heirs to the Habsburg succession if the male line of the Habsburgs became extinct. He had refused to attend the Imperial Diet of 1732, and denied the validity of its decision. France's recognition was given only 'without prejudice to the rights of third parties', an ominous phrase which covered the still more dangerous fact that in 1727 France had concluded a secret treaty with Bavaria, promising to support 'such just claims as the Elector might have on any of the Habsburg dominions' should Charles die without male heirs, and also to support the Elector's candidature for the Imperial Crown.

Moreover, Charles had paid dearly for some of the signatures which he had obtained. To get those of King George of Britain, he had been forced to concede the arrival of Spanish-Bourbon forces in Central Italy and to sacrifice his pet enterprise, his East Indian Trading Company in Ostende. The Elector of Cologne had exacted a considerable cash sum as reward for voting for the Imperial Law of 1732. The Elector of Saxony's guarantee was his price for Austria's support of his candidature for the throne of Poland. France's recognition was part of the general settlement at the end of the War of the Polish Succession, and part-price for her acquisition of Lorraine.

II

While all this was going on over her head, Maria Theresa was growing up—still heiress presumptive, for when, in 1718, Elisabeth bore another child, it was a daughter again—Maria Anna, as was her fourth child, Maria Amalia, born in 1724, and after that, her womb remained closed. Not much is known of the little girl's childhood. It does not seem to have been unhappy. Her father, a pedant for the most rigid Court etiquette, laid stiffness aside in the family circle, where he became simple, kind and affectionate. His wife lacked neither brains nor character, and as a young woman, was a famous beauty, and the two continued to love each other dearly. But

Charles' business of state, and his almost pathological devotion to the chase, left him little time for his family, while his poor consort seems to have been soured by her continued failure to produce the passionately-desired male heir. To stimulate her fertility she took a strange diet which presently completely destroyed her beauty, rendering her, in time, grotesquely stout. In her later writings, Maria Theresa never refers to her. From her 12th year on, her true heart's mother, called by her 'Mami', was her governess, a certain Countess Fuchs, a lady endowed with great good sense, as well as a warm heart. For her Maria Theresa conceived a most deep and enduring affection. 'Die Füchsin' (to translate the term would be to import implications quite lacking in the original, obvious, nickname) remained her friend and confidante (and also her husband's) until her death in 1755, when Maria Theresa paid her the unique honour of having her remains entombed in the Habsburg family vault.

But if not unhappy, the life of the two little girls, Maria Theresa and Marianne (Maria Amalia lived only six years) was far from gay. They seem to have been given few playmates of their own ages, and no surplus of distractions. Their father took them with him on a few outings, such as his annual pilgrimage to Maria Zell and once—fateful occasion—as far afield as Prague, to witness his coronation there. When they grew old enough, they were allowed to attend, and even to perform in, the intimate concerts and ballets which it was one of Charles' pleasures to organise. But most of their time was spent, under the tutelage of 'die Füchsin', either in the private apartments of the sprawling old Hofburg, or, in the summer months, a couple of miles out, in the 'Favoriten', a building later described by an English traveller as 'anything rather than princely, or even commodious, resembling more a nunnery than the habitation of a sovereign.' It was, however, surrounded

5

by extensive parks and gardens; it was there, presumably, that Maria Theresa acquired the passion for fresh air which remained with her all her life. She was, of course, instructed in the polite accomplishments of a young lady: comportment, dancing, singing, in which she was really proficient, the spinet, a little target shooting—but she refused to shoot at living objects. Not riding, which was then considered unladylike; that was a thing which she was to change.

Her tutors, when she came to have them, were Jesuits. From them she received a great deal of religious instruction, which clearly sank in very deep, and a certain amount of history, of a singularly useless kind, names and dates out of the Old Testament and the story of ancient Rome. Questions to which she had to know the answers included: 'how many years did Methuselah live longer than Adam?' and 'in what prose and what verse works do we find accounts of the building of Carthage by Dido?' A good deal of French, especially French as it is written, for although the language which she spoke naturally in later days, using it in her home circle, and in which she probably thought, was a broad Viennese brand of German, she all her life conducted her correspondence, even with her children, in a reasonably correct French, whereas the syntax and even the accidence of her written German are entirely individual, and the vocabulary a bizarre mixture of German, French and Latin. She had some Latin and a little Italian and Spanish, but her instruction in all of these was purely linguistic. There is little evidence that she ever read a non-devotional book for pleasure in her life. Certainly no attempt can ever have been made to inculcate in her a philosophic mind—perhaps fortunately, for so the sterling horse sense might have been blunted which remained her most precious talent.

One thing conspicuously absent from her curriculum

was any sort of preparation for what later destiny made her life's work. Her father seems never truly to have assimilated the thought of a regiment of women. For years he hoped obstinately for a son from Elisabeth, and when it became obvious that this would never be, seems secretly to have hoped to outlive his wife—his general health was far better than hers—and beget an heir by a new consort. At the worst, Maria Theresa should marry and bear a son, who might reach maturity before Charles himself died, and at the very worst, her husband would look after things for a few years. Accordingly, nothing whatever was done to prepare her for any role more active than that of a graceful consort. Her curricula included no instruction in modern European history, except for most misleading panegyrics of her predecessors, none in diplomacy, civics or economics, nor any in the special conditions, problems and aspirations of the peoples who might one day be her subjects, nor was she admitted even to listen to the debates at which decisions on these problems were taken. Charles' outlook is vividly illustrated by the extraordinary fact, recorded below, that when she did marry, he appointed her husband a member of his highest advisory body, the *Geheime Konferenz* (Privy Conference) and President of it in his absence, while not extending the favour of membership to her.

One observer shows her as fretting against this contemptuous treatment. 'She is,' wrote the British Ambassador, 'a princess of the highest spirit. Her father's losses are her own. She reasons already. . . . She admires his virtues but condemns his mismanagement, and is of a temper so formed for rule and ambition as to look on him as little more than her administrator.[1]' But this judgment, although perhaps penetrating, is unique. None of the other glimpses which we have of her as a girl show her as in the least concerned with public affairs as such, nor is

[1] cit: Coxe, *House of Austria* (3rd ed.) III 189.

there any indication that she tried to inform herself on current issues, still less, to acquire any background understanding of them.

For the rest, we have few comments on how her character as a girl struck observers. For her person, we have portraits, which show her as something more than personable. Of medium height, or perhaps a little less, she was then still slender, with well-formed hands and feet, beautiful blue eyes, lovely fair hair, a pure complexion and well-formed, if somewhat determined, features. Even her later enemies admitted the charm and grace of her manner.

She had a remarkable constitution. She was extremely active, could do with abnormally little sleep, and seldom suffered from illness. The lightness with which she took her later pregnancies was phenomenal.

* * *

It may be significant that the occasion of the British Ambassador's remarks on her spirit was one which did indeed involve issues of high policy, but one in which she was following, with the greatest determination, the line dictated by her heart against the whole balance of *raison d'état*. This issue was that of her own marriage. Although in the first years after her birth there was little general expectation that she would become her father's successor, yet Charles' daughter was, even so, a big matrimonial prize, and there was no dearth of applicants for her hand. The King of Portugal, who was the husband of Charles' own sister, suggested his son. A party at Court, headed by Prince Eugene, favoured an alliance with the heir to the Elector of Bavaria (the same who afterwards married Maria Theresa's cousin, Maria Amalia), a match which would have solved the vexed question of Bavaria's claims to the succession. There was even talk of the Crown Prince of Prussia. But Charles had

from the first been especially well-disposed to the suggestions which came from Duke Leopold of Lorraine,
whose father, Charles, had been Prince Eugene's right-
hand man in the great Turkish wars and had then married
the Emperor Leopold's half-sister, while Duke Leopold
himself had grown up with the Emperor Charles, his
childhood's friend as well as his cousin.

Duke Leopold's designs were dogged by ill-luck. His
two eldest sons died in early childhood. The third,
Leopold Clement, was on the point of coming to Austria,
under the pretext of representing his father at Charles'
coronation in Prague, but really to be inspected as Maria
Theresa's bride-groom to be, when he, too, succumbed to
small-pox—this, in June 1723. The elder of the two
surviving boys, Francis Stephen, now his father's heir,
was hurriedly substituted.

Now the spell seemed to have been broken. Francis,
now in his 15th year, was a conspicuously good-looking
lad, of engaging manners. He quite captured the heart of
Charles, who kept him at his Court for 6 years, spent
nominally in study, more often, to his own much greater
pleasure, accompanying Charles on his interminable
hunting expeditions. He was presented to the ladies of
the Court, and later spent many hours in their company.

An unwritten understanding grew up that Maria
Theresa and he were to marry, and child as she was when
it happened—she herself dated the *coup de foudre* at her
first glimpse of him, when she was only six—she very
soon conceived an overmastering passion for him. But
Charles thought the couple too young for a formal
betrothal, and then, as the years passed without bringing
her a brother, Maria Theresa's value on the marriage
market rose; she was becoming a big fish for a mere
prospective Duke of Lorraine. The Queen of Spain
sought her hand for her son. Charles wavered. He did not
like to refuse, for political reasons, but for personal ones

he would not accept. He returned an evasive (and, strictly, rather dishonest) answer, and matters dragged on until the international constellation changed and the match was no longer politically desirable. Then, in 1729, Francis' father died, and he had to go home to take over his heritage; he was away three years on this business, and then touring Europe; his ports of call included Berlin, where he met Frederick, then still Crown Prince, and liked him. When he came back, Charles still could not make up his mind. As a temporary expedient, he appointed Francis Vice-Roy of Hungary, on the face of it no happy inspiration, for the Hungarians, whose jealously-guarded Constitution did not provide for a Vice-Roy, resented it, although afterwards they got to like him, and he them, and it was he who, on Maria Theresa's own later testimony, first disposed her in their favour. Meanwhile, it was easy for him to slip up from Pozsony to court her (this seems to have been one reason why the post was chosen for him) and their love-affair became serious on both sides.

Next, highest hurdle of all, the War of the Polish Succession, breaking out in 1733, produced one of those XVIIIth century balance-of-power imbroglios which had to be settled by dynastic shuffles. In this case, Louis XV reluctantly agreed that Augustus of Saxony should have the Polish Crown if his own nominee, his father-in-law, Stanislas Leszynski, was compensated with Lorraine. Francis was promised the reversion, then clearly imminent, of the Grand Duchy of Tuscany, and it was put to him plainly that unless he renounced Lorraine, the match with Maria Theresa was off: report had it that Bartenstein, the Secretary to the Privy Conference, put the matter to him in the lapidary terms: 'no renunciation, no Archduchess.' He hesitated long, particularly in view of the very strong protests of his mother, who was governing Lorraine for him; the final renunciation was not, indeed, signed until after his wedding. But before that he had given his verbal consent, and been admitted to be Maria Theresa's official suitor. The wedding took place on February 12, 1736.

That so many obstacles had been overcome was a tribute to the vigour with which the young Maria Theresa, supported, indeed, by her mother and 'die Füchsin', had insisted on her way in the face of the hesitations of her father and the strong political opposition of some of his Ministers: an opposition which, given the ideas of the age, was reasonable enough, for the portionless Francis, without money, without soldiers, without influential connections, in 1736 without so much as a throne, even a minor one, was certainly no *parti* for the heiress to the Habsburg dominions. From the personal point of view, nevertheless, the marriage proved an almost unqualified success. Maria Theresa continued to love her husband with a deep and single passion up to his death, and beyond it, when she looked back on her marriage with him as the fount of all her human happiness. His devotion may not have been quite as single-hearted, especially in the later years. Jealous, possessive and at times short-tempered, she cannot have been easy to live with, and rumour credited him with occasional efforts to relax in other company. But his affairs were, at any rate, never publicly scandalous, and the couple's record of 16 children in 19 years shows that he was at least an attentive husband.

Francis had many good qualities, and many talents. He was good-humoured and unpretentious—this, indeed, to a pitch which somewhat shocked the more rigid traditionalists at the Court. Although his spelling was so crude that Maria Theresa herself had to correct it, he was neither a dullard nor a fool. He was far more artistic than his wife, drew and painted, not ill, had an interesting collection of coins, and possessed many curious intellectual interests—amongst others, one in alchemy. Moreover, he had plenty of sound practical sense. When the field was his own, and he had a free hand in it, as in Lorraine when he took it over in 1729 and Tuscany in 1739, he showed himself a wise, kindly and competent ruler.

He was a first-class business man. The relatively modest resources with which he began, the revenues from the Duchy of Teschen (assigned by Charles to his father) and those from Tuscany, were luckily augmented in 1741 by legacies from the widow of his predecessor in Tuscany and from his aunt, the widow of the Elector Palatine, and he invested them with the help of a staff of experts from the Lorraine and Italy, in a remarkable variety of enterprises: real estate, banking (he was said to have money out in most of the leading houses of Europe), State papers, army contracts. His agents' principle seems to have been that money does not smell—at one time during the Seven Years War he was supplying stores to both sides—but the investments were well chosen and productive: he established some of the Monarchy's most modern industries on some of his estates, and on others, model farms; and he ended up with a fortune of over 20 million gulden, in personal estate alone.

Whether the marriage was as successful politically as it was personally is a question which cannot be answered easily. His wife availed herself freely of his special talents. He did valuable service, at the very outset of her reign, in discovering and stopping a number of bizarre leakages which were draining away the Court revenues, and also in curbing her all too numerous fits of impulsive generosity and extravagance. Later, he took over the management of the State debt, into which he introduced a salutory order. In other respects, his role was somewhat inconspicuous. Although she made him 'Co-Regent' with herself, she never understood this as derogating in any way from her own final and absolute authority. When she found his opinion to differ from hers, as it sometimes did on foreign affairs, notably in the first crisis of her reign, and later over the *renversement d'alliances*, she simply swept it aside, and she soon came not even to consult him on administrative and cultural questions, in which he showed little interest. Her elderly councillors treated him with little more respect, which was a pity, for it is very possible that he was right more often than they, or she. He was thus not allowed to be of much help, although he may have contributed more behind the scenes than ever came out. But neither was he any hindrance. With a second opinionated person in them, Maria Theresa's council chambers might have run red with metaphorical blood.

But one virtue which Francis possessed in the highest degree was that of loyalty. Even when he disagreed with his wife, as he certainly did on some important points, notably on the decision to seek alliance with France, which put paid to his hopes of recovering Lorraine, he submitted to being over-ruled. In public he always backed his wife. There was never any question of a Francis party opposing the Queen's party.

It was the more unfortunate that he did not carry self-effacement into the all-important military field. It was, of course, the tradition of the day for royal personages to go campaigning—indeed, they were held to be shirkers or cowards if they did not do so—and when they did, etiquette forbade their being put under the command of non-royalties. Francis burned to win his spurs on the field, and fancied himself as a soldier, but he lacked either the knowledge or the energy and moral courage to impose his will on his subordinates, and his campaigns were inglorious. His wife trembled for his safety every time he went to the wars, but does not seem to have regarded herself as competent to forbid him, nor does she appear ever to have seen through his incapacities, nor those of his hardly more competent brother (to whom, also, she was deeply devoted), Charles of Lorraine. The results were disastrous to the Monarchy, in terms of lost battles, and highly injurious to her own popularity.

This was not the only field in which she allowed her infatuation for her husband to cloud her judgment. We shall see how, on account of it, she came near wrecking her relations with Hungary at the very outset, and it is quite possible that her insistence that, cost what it might, he should have the Imperial Crown, helped to prolong her first big war. Here, moreover, not his personality, but his origin, was really a heavy debit item, for some of the German Princes did not like the idea of a 'French' Emperor, and the debit was very large indeed just in the first years of their marriage. While the French suspected him of intriguing against them in order to recover his old throne, the Austrians, on the contrary, to whom France was at the time Public Enemy No. 1, persisted in regarding him as 'a Frenchman', in league with the national enemy against them.

* * *

The marriage thus aggravated further still the difficulties of what were already the most wretched years of Charles' reign. Since 1733 he had been fighting the unprofitable War of the Polish Succession, and the Preliminary Peace of Vienna of 1735 (made definitive in 1738) had already cost him the bulk of his possessions in Italy. In 1736 Russia, Austria's ally since 1726, was engaged in war with the Porte, and called on Charles for help. The *casus foederis* was doubtful, and Charles began by trying to get the conflict resolved by diplomatic means. But these failed, and pressed by Russia, and also, probably, hoping to compensate himself for his losses in

Italy, Charles agreed to undertake military operations. The General whom he sent down to conduct them, Seckendorf, reported that the conditions, both of the men and the fortresses, were miserable, but Charles insisted on an offensive, and in 1737 the Austrian troops got as far as Nish; but on the Turks rallying, the main force was driven back across the Danube, and Belgrade itself threatened. Still under-estimating the strength of the enemy, and expecting the next year's campaign to end in easy victory, Charles made his son-in-law 'Generalissimus' of it, with Count Königsegg, President of the War Council, as his nominal second in command, but after one or two initial victories, things went worse than ever. Francis soon threw up his commission and returned home, while the Turks pressed forward, winning victory after victory. Königsegg in his turn was superseded, but his successors could do no better. Something like panic seized the Court. On September 1, 1739, Field-Marshal Neipperg, sent down to treat for peace, accepted terms (embodied in a treaty a fortnight later) 'mediated' by France, under which Austria relinquished to the Porte all her gains of 1718 outside the 'historic' frontiers of Hungary.

Of all the many misfortunes which had descended on Charles during his reign, this was the most humiliating, and the most bitter. He himself said that it had taken ten years off his life, and he did not, in fact, long survive it, although his death had no apparent connection with it. His health had not seemed affected, nor his gusto for his favourite diversions diminished. He celebrated his 55th birthday with the usual festivities on October 1, 1740, and a few days later, went on a hunting expedition. On the 9th he was taken violently ill, probably of fungus poisoning, and expired just before dawn on the 20th, bequeathing to his daughter a heritage which was both dismal and highly insecure.

III

In later days it became a favourite occupation of the politicians and historians of the Habsburg Monarchy to argue whether the union between its different components was 'real' or 'personal'. In fact, at most dates in the history of the Monarchy, and certainly in 1740, either was true, according to the angle of vision. With certain minor exceptions relating to very small areas, none of the Habsburgs had ever attempted to establish any organised political unity between the innumerable domains, great or small, which inheritance, purchase, exchange, or, more rarely, conquest, had brought under their rule: each had remained the 'historic-political unit' as which it had entered into that condition, with its own institutions, which were not necessarily the same in any two of them, and its own direct and individual relationship to its *Landesherr*, who was King here, Duke there, Count there. The Pragmatic Sanction did not alter this mutual independence of the Provinces (as it will be convenient to call them, although some of them rejected the term as derogatory to their dignity), and so far as their internal affairs were concerned, he dealt (in theory) with each of them separately.

On the other hand, he possessed in all of them the prerogatives of ordering their foreign relations and their defence system. In these respects, i.e., in respect of their relations with the outer world, they constituted a unit. His monarchic privileges further entitled him to the yield of the mines of precious metals and salt, that of customs dues, and of certain indirect and special taxes. The Crown also possessed properties, some of them considerable, in nearly every Province.

The political structure of the Monarchy was, accordingly, dualistic. The Monarch exercised his sovereign prerogatives, in respect of which his powers were absolute, through central authorities, responsible to himself alone. Foreign affairs, or rather, most of them, were conducted by the titular head of the Austrian Court Chancellery, described below.[1] The supreme military instance was the *Hofkriegsrat* (Court War Council), which also acted as a General Staff. Its other duties were administrative and judicial. The 'Q Branch' was in the hands of a separate body, the *Generalkriegskommissariat* (General War Commissariat), which also drew up the military budget.

The collection and administration of the Crown Revenues was the charge of the *Hofkammer*, or 'Camera', in practice another central and Monarchy-wide institution; the Hungarian 'Camera' was technically a separate body, but the Hungarian Diet had no control over its operations. There were also two central financial bodies, a *Ministerialbankodeputation*, which looked after the State credit, operating in practice through the *Wiener Stadt-bank* (Vienna City Bank), the only financial institution in the Monarchy which had been able to capture the public confidence, and the *Universalbankalität*, a sort of State rival of the Vienna City Bank. A *Finanzkonferenz* was supposed to co-ordinate the work of these bodies.

Outside these fields, the Monarch shared his authority in each Province with its local 'organs of self-government', which almost everywhere were in the form of 'Estates', usually composed of the local Lords Spiritual and Temporal, representatives of the lesser nobility, and, of grace, one or two representatives of the local Royal Free Boroughs. In Hungary the representatives of the smaller nobles, two from each County, constituted a separate 'Table' and the constitution of Transylvania was peculiar.

[1] Since the initiation of this practice, there had been two 'Austrian Court Chancellors', the senior (in practice) the Foreign Minister, while the second looked after the real agenda of the Austrian Provinces.

The Monarch corresponded with the Estates through secretariats, or Chancelleries, of which, indeed, it had not been found necessary to maintain a separate one for each Province. In 1740 there were four Chancelleries: the 'Austrian', for the so-called German Austrian Provinces and the 'Vorlande' (the outlying western enclaves) and Imperial affairs, the 'Bohemian', for the Lands of the Bohemian Crown (Bohemia, Moravia and Silesia), the 'Hungarian', for the Kingdom of Hungary and Croatia, and the Transylvanian. The senior of the two 'Austrian' Chancellors looked after foreign affairs, and ranked as the senior Minister of the Monarchy. The Italian Provinces and the Netherlands had their own 'Councils'. The 'Military Frontier', a long, narrow defensive strip running the length of the Turkish frontier, and the Bánát of Temesvár, comprising the territory recovered from the Porte in 1725 and not re-ceded in 1739, were administered through the War Council and the Camera.

The powers of the Estates had been sapped during the preceding decades and centuries, and it was only in Hungary that they were still at all far-reaching. There the Monarch was not entitled to enact legislation except in agreement with the Diet, which he was pledged to convoke at least every three years. The national rights and privileges which on coronation he swore to respect were also relatively extensive. Everywhere else he had the right of enacting legislation, and the Estates' prescriptive rights were more modest, but they were often not negligible. Moreover, the administration in every Province was conducted by and through the Estates, which also usually acted as executants of the Monarch's will when he was acting in exercise of his supreme prerogatives.

The point at which the two net-works of authority intersected was that of finance, and in particular, military finance. In earlier times the Monarch had been supposed to 'live of his own', which was not quite impracticable when his armies were composed of levies drawn from each Province. If he needed more money for any purpose, he asked the Estates of one or more Provinces for a *contributio*. This was an extraordinary tax, and the Estates were entitled to refuse it. With the change-over to standing armies, the levies had become obsolete, and the Provinces, except Hungary, the Military Frontier and the Tirol, were no longer required to provide personal service. Against this, the *contributio* had become a regular tax, which was apportioned among the Provinces in rough proportion to their presumed taxable capacity. Since the XVIIth century it had become an unwritten law that the army was kept up out of the *contributio*, while the Crown's remaining expenditure (on the Court, the central services and the foreign missions) was met out of the 'cameral' resources.

The Provincial Estates derived about three quarters of the money out of which they paid the *contributio* from a land tax, which was levied only on peasant-cultivated holdings, the nobles having preserved the exemption of their demesne lands from such taxation which had formerly been granted them as equivalent for their old obligation to perform military service. As, however, they had to budget also for their own internal services, the yield of the land tax seldom met all their requirements, and a proportion—usually about a quarter—of their revenues was derived from minor taxes, direct or indirect.

Many of these institutions were centuries old; few of them had been modernised within living memory, and hardly any of them co-ordinated with one another. Conflicts of competence and mutual jealousies, both inter-departmental and inter-regional, abounded. The great top-level battle was between the central authorities and the provincial Estates, the former complaining that they were obstructed and starved, and that the Estates, while moaning over the tyrannous burden of the *contributio*, spent vast sums on wasteful administration, inordinately high salaries for their own staffs, and even corrupt *douceurs*; while the latter said that they were squeezed for purposes that were of no profit or interest to them (and there was a good deal to be said for each of these cases—more for the latter than had generally been admitted by later Austrian historians, centralist-minded middle-class 'progressives' to a man as they have been). The position of the Provinces was in practice much stronger than it looked to be on paper (outside Hungary), because the Crown's own services, including the Chancelleries, were staffed with members of the families represented on the Estates, top posts being held, by prescriptive tradition, by members of the high local aristocracies, and thus probably brothers or cousins of those provincial petty kings whom Maria Theresa describes bitterly as 'capi' ('heads').

But each main opposing camp was also the prey to intestine strife. Each Province did its best to push all possible burdens onto the shoulders of the others. The War Council, strangely, was responsible for relations with Russia and the Porte; on the other hand, it was not exclusively competent even in the restricted field left to it by the existence of the General Commissariat, for there still existed two sub-War Councils, in Graz and Innsbruck respectively, with considerable local powers. The General Commissariat was responsible partly to the War Council, partly to the Camera, and ceaselessly at war with both; a 'Deputation' which was supposed to coordinate the operations of the three bodies never came within eye-shot of harmonising them. The Camera was the common enemy of every other organisation.

The effects of this system, or lack of system, were devastatingly apparent in the condition of the public services. If danger came, Maria Theresa would need, as Prince

Eugene had warned her father, a full purse and a strong army. Charles had left her neither. The army had deteriorated with astonishing rapidity since Prince Eugene's grip on it had loosened. The losses incurred in the recent wars had not been made up, and even further reductions made, for economy's sake. Of the nominal strength of 160,000 men, hardly more than 80,000 were under arms, to defend frontiers reaching from those of the Netherlands and Parma, to those of Turkey; the bulk of them, including almost all the cavalry, were in Hungary. There were only 40 pieces of artillery. The men were stationed in small groups, sometimes only two or three in a village, making administration difficult and the growth of any esprit de corps impossible. The rank and file were poor devils, ill-equipped and paid, many of them impressed by dubious means, and kept from desertion, which even so was rife, only by inhuman penalties. Every regiment had its own drill and training. Among the officers, promotion went largely by favour or purchase, partly official: a Field-Marshal-Lieutenant had to pay 1,000 gulden to become a Field-Marshal. Commands of regiments were bought and sold between individuals. Most of the holders of higher ranks were self-indulgent dilettantes, and nearly all of them utterly consumed by mutual jealousies. The subalterns, their scanty pay often in arrears, were dejected and disgruntled. The fortresses were generally in disrepair, and scanty: Prague was the only fortified place in Bohemia.

The condition of the State finances was lamentable. Charles had not been the first extravagant member of his family. Generations of his forebears had poured out the resources of the State on dynastic wars or on the maintenance of sumptuous Courts—Leopold I had spent about 50,000 gulden a year on the purchase of jewels, and operas, ballets and gala festivities had swallowed immense sums—or on purposes less selfish but equally nonproductive, such as donations to favourites or to the Church, the latter so lavish that Maria Theresa herself, devoted daughter of the Church as she was, warned her children against continuing them. To raise these sums, the Crown's cameral resources had been given away or farmed out, usually for sums far below their real value. The *contributio* which should have supplemented these had to be wrung, sometimes year by year, out of the reluctant Estates, some of which were heavily in arrears with it. Especially since the loss of Naples-Sicily, this, too, had been yielding sums barely adequate to cover expenditure in time of peace, let alone war. In 1736 the State had nevertheless been able to budget for revenues of nearly 40 million gulden, but receipts had subsequently sunk to little over half that figure, against greatly increased expenditure. The State was driven increasingly to cover its deficit by borrowing from public or private lenders, and on her accession, Maria Theresa found herself confronted with a public debt of 100 million gulden (it had been 60.5 at the beginning of her father's reign), including an advance from the Bank of England of £320,000, repayable in annual quotas beginning in 1743, while in her treasury she had no more than 70,000 gulden.

* * *

The picture was little brighter outside the central services. In most of the Provinces, the Estates had become the preserves of the local great landed magnates, who dominated them to the exclusion not only of the peasants, who were entirely unrepresented, and the Free Boroughs, practically so, but even of the lesser nobility, for whom the preceding two centuries had been a period of decay; it was only in Hungary that they still constituted anything of a force. The rule of these magnates, who in each Province formed small inter-related cliques, was a thoroughly selfish one. Concerned only for the advance-

ment of themselves and their families, they squeezed the
last drop of sweat from their peasants and thwarted the
development of the towns and of industry, lest it should
draw away workers from their lands.

* * *

The things of which, as she wrote afterwards, Maria
Theresa found herself lacking on her accession included,
besides money, soldiers and personal experience,
'counsel'. The Monarch's advisory body of the day, the
latest edition of a long line of experiments, was the
Geheimer Konferenz (Privy Conference), an assem-
blage of a maximum of eight members, chosen by the
Monarch at his discretion, although the heads of the
central services were always included.[1] Charles had let it
run down, as he had most things, and when he died it
comprised only five members, not counting his son-in-
law, whom shortly before he had designated to replace
him if he was absent. Its senior member was Count
Ludwig Sinzendorf, Austrian Court Chancellor and,
under the system of the day, responsible for the Ministry's
foreign relations. He had held that post for many years
and gave himself airs which apparently over-awed Maria
Theresa, who describes him as 'a great statesman', but it
cannot be said that his record, seen in retrospect, is
particularly brilliant. In any case he had by this time—
he was now in his 70th year—lost most of such energy
and elasticity as he had ever possessed. He was, moreover, financially corrupt to such a degree as to make it a
complete riddle why—since the fact was notorious—
Charles had allowed him to remain in office; and Maria
Theresa herself writes that she never trusted him.

The man next to him in seniority was Count Gun-
dacker Starhemberg, President of the *Hofkammer* and

[1] In the Monarch's absence, his 'Lord Marshal' (*Oberst-
kämmerer*) took the chair for him.

founder of the City Bank of Vienna, over the operations of which he had presided for many years with success and complete integrity. Him she did trust, as 'a great man and an upright German', but admits that he had not so much political insight as Sinzendorf, whom he even exceeded in years: he was 77.

The pen need not linger at all over the other three. Count Alois Harrach, *Landmarschall* of Lower Austria, was a respectable and honourable, but intellectually mediocre, ex-diplomat who had served as Vice-Roy of Naples from 1728 to 1733. His brother, Count Joseph Harrach, had been promoted to the Presidency of the War Council when its previous holder, Königsegg, was relieved of it to take charge of the campaign against the Turks—because, Charles had said frankly, 'there was no great choice.' Finally, Königsegg had been allowed to keep his seat in the Conference as consolation for losing the other appointment. The ages of the three were respectively 72, 69 and 67.

Far more really important than any of them was the *Referendar* or Secretary to the Conference, Johann Christoph Bartenstein. The son of a Protestant University Professor of Strasbourg, Bartenstein had come to Austria as a young man to tutor the children of a noble family, turned Catholic and entered the service of the Lower Austrian Estates; he had been picked out for his post in 1730. Nominally, his duties were only to take the minutes of the Conference, but as Charles seldom troubled to attend the meetings of that body, contenting himself with receiving reports of its meetings, he came to see much of the secretary and took to using him as his own channel of communications, written and oral, not only with the Conference but also with his own representatives abroad and with those of foreign Powers in Vienna, so that all threads ran together in Bartenstein's hands.

Very able and prodigiously industrious, Bartenstein

acquired an encyclopaedic knowledge of the affairs of the Monarchy, to the welfare of which he was completely devoted. This, however, he coupled with an aggressive self-assertiveness which his didactic manner and his verbosity made the more unpleasing. It goes without saying that the enemies of this bourgeois parvenu and intruder were innumerable, and Maria Theresa herself was, as she confesses, at first 'right ill prejudiced against him', probably for his abrupt treatment of Francis over the renunciation of Lorraine. Later she came to appreciate his qualities and to esteem and rely on him, although this never blinded her to his faults of temperament.

* * *

The economic and cultural backwardness of the Monarchy matched its political confusion. Since the banishing of the Turkish danger in 1683, the reconciliation with Hungary in 1713, and the almost simultaneous ceasing of the plague to be a ravage, Vienna had blossomed like a rose. It was the age of High Baroque, which found splendid expression in the capital of the Empire and of Europe's largest state, the meeting-place of architects and artists from Germany, Italy, the Netherlands, Spain. Splendid churches and palaces in the new mode overshadowed its narrow streets, and were spreading outside them, the greatest of all, Prince Eugene's magnificent Belvedere Palace and the still unfinished summer residence of the Imperial family at Schönbrunn. The Provinces also contained their share of sumptuous monasteries and palaces, for it was the pride of the great men of the day (who often ruined themselves in satisfying it) to outbuild their neighbours.

But the gaiety and luxury of the capital were largely a façade. Outside it, standards had indeed risen in the previous generation, with the absence of plague and of war (for Charles' wars had nearly all been fought abroad), but economic conditions everywhere in the Monarchy, outside the Netherlands and Italy, were still very backward. Vienna, and, a long way after it, Prague, were the only towns considerable by modern standards. Charles, who was no fool in such matters, had done a good deal to improve main communications and had made attempts, in the mercantilist philosophy of the day, to promote industry and commerce, but for various reasons, not least the jealousy of the landlords, these had made little progress. Most luxury articles were still imported, mainly from France, and the market for these did not extend far outside the Court. Even in the more prosperous Austrian and Bohemian Provinces, 'industry' was still mainly in the hands of small craftsmen, organised in guilds and working for the local market; only Silesian linen, Bohemian glass and Styrian iron sent their products further afield. The great depopulated expanses of central and southern Hungary could hardly show so much as a craftsman; there the peasant families formed autarkic economic units. The great bulk of the population derived its livelihood from agriculture, generally carried on by methods which had changed little since the Middle Ages. Most of the peasants, moreover, were villeins, not technically serfs but largely at the mercy of the men who were at once their landlords and the representatives and executants of authority over them, and whose economic yoke had been growing steadily heavier for a century past.

* * *

Aristocratic visitors to Vienna were impressed, not only by its architecture, but also by the operas, concerts and theatrical performances which they saw there, and these were indeed refined and luxurious enough: Charles himself was a great patron of the arts, and a dabbler in them: he sometimes conducted an orchestra, and had himself composed an opera. But these performances existed for the delectation of the Court; many of them were given for the Imperial family and its guests. A few great magnates aped them, but below that level there was nothing till one came to the strolling players, mummers and bear-baiters who provided amusement for the 'lower classes'.

The only Church 'tolerated' in most Provinces of the Monarchy was the Catholic: only in Transylvania and parts of Hungary did the Protestants enjoy a limited 'toleration', as did the recently-immigrated Serbs of the Military Frontier; elsewhere, non-Catholics were still liable to expulsion. Almost all education was in the hands of the Churches, i.e., outside the handful of Protestant foundations in the areas mentioned (the Orthodox populations did without schooling), those of the Catholic Church. The Jesuits had gradually taken over the Universities until almost all the teaching in them, except of medicine and (in part) of law was done by them. The secondary schools were maintained, controlled and staffed by various Orders, Jesuits, Benedictines, Piarists and others. The primary schools were often maintained by the manorial lords, but the teacher was usually the village parson or his assistant, the sexton-verger.

The standard of instruction in most of these institutions had sunk to a very low level. The methods of the Jesuits were cumbersome and antiquated, their teaching, almost all in Latin, their curricula narrow and unpractical. Teaching in subjects outside theology had become so inefficient that most serious students went abroad to complete their studies. The rich kept private tutors for their sons. It was often possible to obtain a degree by simple bribery. The teaching in the secondary schools, almost all of which were *gymnasia*, was again mostly in Latin, and its object, to inculcate the true faith and to train the next generation of priests. The village schools were rudimentary and also very thin on the ground, especially in the non-German areas.

IV

Perhaps the most dangerous element in the whole situation was the wide-spread disaffection among the Monarchy's own peoples. Even before the unhappy Turkish War, Charles had not been popular among his subjects. He had not been detested for a tyrant, and, indeed, he was none, but the specific grievances of certain Provinces apart—and Hungary, in particular, had accumulated a long tally of legitimate grievances, justly resented—there had been much grumbling at the extravagance of his sumptuous Court, and behind all this, a lack of positive enthusiasm for his rule which was largely of his own making, the result of his complete failure, sensed by his peoples, to identify himself spiritually with them. His conception of his position was purely dynastic, one which regarded his peoples as pawns in the game of balance, not of the power of States, but of the glory of dynasties. His Austrian Provinces were not even those nearest to his heart: he had never overcome his early fixation on Spain, and when driven thence, he had surrounded himself, for preference, with Spanish hangers -on. Vienna, under his sway, was less a German Court than a Spain or a Naples in exile. The presence of these 'Spanish leeches' had been doubly resented since the loss of Naples in 1735, after which the whole cost of their maintenance had fallen on Charles' German subjects.

Charles' peoples reacted to his attitude each as its own feelings prompted it, for there was as yet not the smallest feeling of mutual cohesion or attachment between one Province and another: or not, at least, between the different groups of Provinces. But all felt this much: if they had to be the mere subjects of a ruler, why should that ruler be this haughty, Spaniard-minded man? The Hungarians, the least satisfied with their actual condi-

28

tion, were perhaps on the whole the least anxious for a fundamental change, for they still needed help to protect them against the Turks. But among the Germans and in Bohemia, where the Germanised aristocracy spoke for the country, there were many who would positively have preferred the Wittelsbach, who was at least a German, and husband of a wife who was herself a Habsburg, and that of a line senior to Maria Theresa's.

Disaffection, endemic but previously not acute, had been made active and acute by the fiascos of the Turkish War. More blood spilt, more treasure wasted, and above all, territorial losses which this time went to the quick. Austrians (and Hungarians) did not mind if Naples and Sicily were lost, but it was a different thing to see the glory reaped by Prince Eugene squandered and the Turkish danger, thought to have been banished for ever, suddenly back again. The military débâcles of 1738 and still more, the humiliating peace of 1739, had roused real storms of resentment against those held responsible; soldiers had had to be called out to protect some of them from lynching.

Charles had made scape-goats of his generals: he had had the two leading figures at the end, Neipperg and Wallis, as well as Seckendorf, degraded and imprisoned. But the hostility had not spared Charles himself, and still less had it spared his son-in-law.

Francis' part in the events had, indeed, been unfortunate. He had expected to be given a dignified and lucrative post on his marriage, but for a long year after it, although promising him the eventual Governorship of the Netherlands, Charles had kept him hanging about without an appointment or even an establishment of his own: the young couple were given a modest appanage, but resided in the Hofburg. Francis then decided to win laurels for himself in the field, and in June 1737 set out for the Front as a 'volunteer', taking his brother with him. The two young men proved much more trouble than they were worth. Francis took with him a suite which included three Chamberlains, a secretary, a father confessor, three doctors, three valets, eight cooks and four scullions, and an enormous baggage-train, the freight of which included a supply of drinking-water from the Viennese hills. Then he nearly got taken prisoner, out hunting bears.

Meanwhile, the last Medici Grand Duke of Tuscany had died. The throne was Francis', and everyone who wanted him out of the way urged him to go down and take possession of it. He did not want to be away from the centre of things, and in December Charles suddenly (no-one really knows why) changed his policy towards him, appointing him a member of his Privy Conference (to preside over it in his own absence) and, as has been said, 'Generalissimus' for the 1738 campaign.

As we have said, he soon resigned his command, and handed back another commission, to treat for peace with the Turks, even faster. His attitude is quite intelligible, for he had been given impossible instructions, having been told always to accept the majority view of a Council of War, and he had refused to cover a decision with which he had disagreed. He may have been right in his view, and he was certainly not to be blamed for the débâcle which followed after he was outvoted. But public opinion, nevertheless, put the responsibility for it on him.

Meanwhile, he had aggravated his unpopularity by bringing with him a cortège of courtiers from Lorraine, eyed askance by the Viennese as another set of foreign leeches.

As for Maria Theresa, no one knew anything about her, and no one expected her to be in the least important. Obscure domesticity was to be her lot; her function, to bear Charles a grandson. And in this she had, up to date, failed. Her first child, born on February 2, 1737, had been a daughter (Maria Elisabeth), as was her second, Maria Anna, born on June 10, 1738.

At the end of 1738 Francis was after all sent down to be installed in Tuscany. The young couple (Maria Theresa went with him) set out in December, arriving in Florence, after a wearisome journey which included a fortnight's quarantine on the Venetian frontier, in January 1739.

Politically, the visit went off well. Francis' good sense and conciliatory conduct pleased his new subjects: his wife's youthful radiance captivated them. On her unromantic and inartistic soul, however, the journey, the longest of her life, the only occasion in it on which she ever set foot on foreign soil, except when she went to Frankfurt to see her husband crowned Emperor, ever saw the South (she never saw Milan again, nor for that matter, Brussels ever), or the sea (on a day-trip to Leghorn), seems to have made no impression whatever. She fretted for news of her children, and the only feeling which curbed her impatience to be back home with them was the fear that her husband would go dashing off to the wars again.

In fact, when they got back to Vienna at the end of May, he wanted to do so, but this time Charles refused him leave. Francis was thus guiltless also of the humiliating terms of peace, but again, public opinion made him the culprit. Neipperg had been his tutor, and was known to be his friend, and rumour had it that 'the Frenchman' and his wife had secretly instructed the General to conclude the disgraceful transaction.

So the young couple had to drag out another year of obscurity and unpopularity, which had not abated when Charles died.

PART TWO

THE YOUNG QUEEN
1740–1756

I

This was the situation in which Maria Theresa was suddenly called upon to undertake her enormous responsibilities: to do so at the age of 23, almost unwarned and entirely unprepared, and into the bargain, once again with child. She met it with calm, dignity and surprising maturity. On the evening of her father's death, she received the chief Court dignitaries and Ministers, and confirmed them in their offices. The next day, she presided over a meeting—her first—of the Privy Conference, her husband seated at her left hand. She spoke to them in affecting terms of the loss which she had suffered, but also of her determination to defend her rights. She took one other step of immediate importance: on November 21 she appointed her husband co-Regent with her, and guardian of her children should she die before her heir came of age; but for the rest, she deferred making any changes until she should have learned something of the business of government.

At first it seemed likely that she would get the breathing-space which she needed. The Bavarian Minister put in formal notification of his Monarch's claim to the throne, but Sinzendorf produced the original document, which showed the claim to be unfounded: it spoke of the extinction, not of 'the male line', as the Bavarian copy had it, but of 'legitimate issue'. It was supposed that this settled the question, and in the next few weeks, Britain, the Netherlands, Sardinia, the Holy See and Venice announced their acceptance of Maria Theresa's accession. France made excuses for not formally acknowledging the notification of it sent to Versailles, but did not declare non-recognition of it. The Porte had not yet ratified the Peace of Belgrade, but seemed disposed to keep it.

In the first weeks there had been demonstrations and food riots in Vienna, after storms had ruined the vintage and the game preserved by Charles for his pleasure had been wreaking havoc in the peasants' plots; also a continuance of the demonstrations against the War Council. But the immediate discontent was appeased by some sensible remedial measures suggested, it appears, by Francis (the peasants were allowed to shoot off the game, and some relief was distributed), and Maria Theresa's charm and affability disarmed the Estates when they came to make obeisance to her. When, on March 13, she was delivered of another child, and it proved to be, at last, a boy (it was the later Joseph II) her stock rose with a bound among the volatile Viennese and even her husband came in for his share of credit.

Another pleasant episode of the winter was the arrival of a picturesque mission from the Sultan, bearing the instruments of ratification of the Treaty of Belgrade.

But meanwhile, a bolt had fallen from the blue, and that from a totally unexpected quarter. Frederick of Prussia, invoking as pretext a historical claim which his own advisers declared invalid, and to which he himself attached not the slightest importance, prepared to grab Silesia. While already mobilising, he sent an emissary to Vienna, representing himself as Maria Theresa's friend and offering her, in return for cession of the Duchy, his guarantee of the rest of her dominions against any other claimant, a cash payment of two million thaler and his vote for Francis at the forthcoming Imperial election.

This was the first great crisis of Maria Theresa's reign, and her first great individual moment. Several of her councillors, including Sinzendorf—in the main, those who took the danger from France more seriously (and, it must be added, appreciated its magnitude more exactly) —advised 'negotiation', which must have meant at least partial surrender. Francis himself, well-disposed towards Frederick and presumably tempted by the prospect of the Imperial crown, wavered. Only Starhemberg and Bartenstein took the other side. It has been argued that the party of surrender were right, and Frederick's terms were in fact what Maria Theresa was forced to accept after 7, and indeed 14, years of fighting—although the argument rests on the highly questionable assumption that Frederick would later have kept his word. But Maria Theresa, who all her life was as resolute in defending her own rights as she was scrupulous in respecting those of others, would not hear of surrender. She over-rode the opposition, including that of her husband (when he showed signs of yielding to the Prussian envoy's representations, she interrupted the conversation, telling him that dinner was waiting), and sent back an uncompromising refusal: 'Never, never, will the Queen renounce an inch of all her hereditary Lands, though she perish with all that remains to her. Rather the Turks in front of Vienna, rather cession of the Netherlands to France, rather any concession to Bavaria and Saxony, than renunciation of Silesia!'

Meanwhile, Frederick had begun to move even before the irrevocable reply was delivered: his troops crossed the frontier on December 16. The Province had only a couple of fortresses in it, and was otherwise as good as undefended. He had over-run almost all of it in a matter of days, rather than weeks: Breslau opened its gates to him on January 3. There his troops halted, while Maria Theresa made her preparations to drive them out when the fighting season should open (for the armies of that day still, like Julius Caesar's, went into winter quarters).

Had those preparations been adequate, the whole later course of history might well have been different, for that winter Europe was waiting to see which way the cat would jump. Cardinal Fleury had sent Marshal Belle-Isle on a tour of the German Electoral Courts to collect votes for the Elector of Bavaria to succeed Charles, but this was no act of war, and had the Austrian armies beaten Frederick's, France might well have gone no further. Unhappily for Maria Theresa, the army which met Frederick's at Mollwitz, on April 10, 1741, was a weak force under an untalented and dilatory commanding officer—F.M. Neipperg, who with his fellow victims had been pardoned and rehabilitated.[1] Even so, it came within a hairbreadth of succeeding, and thus justifying Maria Theresa's resolve: the Austrian cavalry opened the action with a charge so dashing that Frederick himself believed the day lost and ran away ingloriously. But the well-drilled Prussian infantry rallied and counter-attacked, and the end was, after all, a victory for Prussia.

The news was a disappointment to Maria Theresa, but not a crushing blow, for the defeat had not been heavy, and she hoped to repair it. She found time to write Neipperg a comforting letter in the middle of her preparations for what was to prove in the event the first major internal political struggle of her reign. A deputation had arrived from Hungary to remind her that until crowned in due form, she was not the country's legal ruler; and a coronation in Hungary was no empty ceremony. The Monarch undergoing it was required to swear to respect the national rights and liberties, and to

[1] Wallis refused further service. Seckendorf actually went across and took service under the Elector of Bavaria.

35

sign a Diploma in which they were summarised. This was done at a Diet at which the relations between Crown and Nation were restated, the Monarch first presenting his 'propositions' then receiving the nation's *gravamina*, as the Diet's requests were traditionally called. Left by Charles unconvoked for many years of essentially unconstitutional rule, the Hungarians had accumulated a formidable back-log of *gravamina*, of which the Diet, when it met on May 18, began to draw up a list; they also wanted the Coronation Diploma amended to make the guarantee of the national liberties more extensive and more specific.

Here, too, Maria Theresa seems at first entirely to have under-estimated the seriousness of the problem. She herself knew nothing of Hungarian constitutional history, and her advisers were, almost to a man, men of the old, centralist school, who knew as little, and were deeply hostile to all Hungarian pretensions whatever. The reply which they drew up for her refused flatly to alter the Diploma, and she declared that she did not propose to bargain over her 'propositions', the first of which was that her husband should be crowned co-Regent with her. This the Diet refused as strongly, and hard words were exchanged before she agreed to drop the coronation of Francis and they to accept an unaltered wording of the Diploma in return for a promise that their legitimate grievances should be properly considered after the coronation.

Now Maria Theresa set out for Pozsony, and was duly crowned on June 25 with the traditional pompous ritual (which Francis watched as a spectator: he was not even given a place in the official cortège). She played her part with grace and dignity: the Holy Crown of St. Stephen on her head, his cloak over her shoulders, she galloped her horse (she had learned to ride for the occasion) up to the summit of the Coronation Hill and pointed the sword of St. Stephen towards the four quarters in token of her determination to defend the land against attack coming from any of them.

But this done, the real trouble commenced. When, on July 28, the Royal reply to the *gravamina* was read out, it was received by the Lower Table—the representatives of the untitled nobility—with 'scornful laughter and a wild din of half-represssed cries of rage'; and this was fully understandable, for practically every one of the requests was either rejected outright, or accepted with such reservations and limitations as were tantamount to refusal. It was a large-scale domestic crisis, and it coincided with the full impact of the international one.

If Mollwitz had been no heavy military defeat for the Austrian arms, its political consequences had been enormous. It had encouraged all Austria's enemies in their designs on her. At the end of May France, Spain and Bavaria concluded the Treaties of Nymphenburg. The two larger Powers were to help the Elector of Bavaria with troops and money to secure him possession of the Imperial Crown and of the Austrian territories claimed by him (Bohemia and most of the Alpine Provinces); they in return were to keep any territories conquered by their armies, including the Austrian Netherlands for France, and Austria's Italian possessions for Spain. A fortnight later, Frederick adhered to the Treaty; his share was to be Silesia.

It was practically Austria *contra mundum*, for Russia, although an ally since 1726, was too preoccupied with internal dissension, and with a threat from Sweden, to help. Saxony was wavering. There remained only Britain, whose interest in the maintenance of the balance of power gave her a natural community of purpose with Austria, and who was, indeed, already engaged in a war, declared a year before, with Spain—now almost France's client—over that issue of overseas trade which was the sensitive point of her relations with France. But Britain's foreign policy was still in the hands of Walpole, a man of peace on principle—it was only with reluctance that he had declared war on Spain—and particularly anxious to avoid a major clash with France, in view of the situation in Scotland. Moreover, Britain had in 1725 concluded an alliance with Prussia—this in the interest of the freedom of the Baltic—and was thus in the difficult position of being contractually engaged to both parties to the Silesian dispute. Finally, King George feared for the safety of his Electorate of Hanover, should Frederick turn against it.

Consequently, although there was sympathy enough for Maria Theresa in London, Walpole decided that Britain's best policy was to attempt to keep the potential enemies of France in line by negotiating settlements between them. Maria Theresa had appealed to Britain as soon as Frederick invaded Silesia. The British Government sent no answer at all until April, when Robinson was empowered to say that if Austria chose war with Prussia, Britain would fulfil her obligations as guarantor of the Pragmatic Sanction by sending a force of 12,000 men (these were to be troops hired from Denmark and Hesse) and providing a subsidy of £300,000; but he was to represent the dangers of the situation, and to advise Maria Theresa to sacrifice Lower Silesia, with Breslau.

Robinson made representations to this effect on various occasions, while Lord Hyndford went to Berlin to press Frederick to abate his price. Both Frederick and Maria Theresa refused all offers. Then came the agreements of Nymphenburg, enhancing King George's fears for his Electorate, which he now saw threatened with invasion from France. On July 24 Robinson, the British Ambassador, arrived in Pozsony with the news (which had not yet reached Austria) of the formation of the hostile coalition, and the intimation that in this situation, while the subsidy would be paid as promised, no troops would be supplied. Indeed, King George, *qua* Elector, signed a Treat of Neutrality with France, undertook to give Austria no military aid, and promised his electoral vote to Bavaria.

Robinson pressed the Queen in the strongest possible terms to pay Frederick his price, and now all her advisers, even Bartenstein, urged her to yield. For weeks she held out with an obstinacy which aroused in Robinson admiration, exasperation and personal fear of her tongue, in equal proportions. She sent him to Frederick with a compromise offer which the Prussian rejected scornfully. She made large offers to France, and overtures to Bavaria through her uncle's widow, the Dowager Empress Amalia. All were rejected, and meanwhile, on July 31, Charles Albert seized Passau, and in mid-August French troops, wearing Bavarian cockades, crossed the Rhine. At last, on September 8, Maria Theresa signed a document offering Frederick Lower Silesia if he would renounce the French alliance and vote for her husband as Emperor; more, if he would actually join the alliance against France and Bavaria. '*Placet*,' she wrote on Sinzendorf's draft, 'since there is no other help, but to my extreme grief.'

But meanwhile she had made up her mind to take a bold step.

The Monarchy still had in Hungary a great, untapped source of military man-power, but the Austrian Ministers, fixed in their belief that the Hungarians were incorrigible rebels, had been against drawing on it, out of fear that if given arms, the Hungarians would turn them against the Monarchy. Possibly influenced by her husband,[1] Maria Theresa decided to take the risk. On September 11 she called the whole Diet to the castle to

---

[1] A note was found in her papers after her death that it was Francis who 'had taught her to love the Hungarians.'

receive a personal message from her. The Holy Crown on her head, her fair beauty enhanced by the mourning which she was still wearing for her father, she depicted to them the extreme peril in which her throne stood, and appealed to them in moving terms for their help, placing herself under their protection; and they in return intoned the traditional formula of the proclamation of the noble *insurrectio*: 'Life and blood for our King, Maria Theresa.'

The famous scene was neither quite so spontaneous, nor so sentimental, as later legend has represented it. Before confronting the full Diet, Maria Theresa had consulted a small group of magnates trusted by her, and they at least organised and led the chorus of assent. But these historical truths do not detract from the boldness of Maria Theresa's resolution, nor the artistry with which she carried it through; nor, for that matter, the genuine, if transient, quality of the chivalrous devotion which she succeeded in awakening in the hard-boiled Hungarian squires.

It was by no means the end of the constitutional struggle. The Diet did not rise until October 29, and the intervening weeks saw much unsentimental bargaining. The Diet did, however, in return for considerable concessions, which included the 'inarticulation' (i.e., formal registration) as a 'fundamental law' of noble exemption from taxation, agree to supplement the levy with a further 32,000 men from the unfree population, raising the total military contribution from the Lands of the Hungarian Crown to the figure of some 100,000 men. It even accepted Francis as co-Regent—though on terms which made the office little more than nominal. When he appeared, on September 21, to take the oath to the Constitution, his wife accompanied him, bearing in her arms her infant boy and destined successor (looking 'much like a squirrel') who gave a squeak at the appropriate moment. He said later that his mother had pinched his bottom.

Meanwhile, things had begun by going from bad to worse in the West. The Elector of Saxony, who in April had signed a Treaty of Alliance with Austria (it had, it is true, not been ratified), changed sides and joined the enemy coalition in return for a promise of Moravia and other territories. Maria Theresa would have been left with Inner Austria and Hungary. Charles Albert, his advance practically unopposed, entered Linz on September 21 and on October 2 received the homage, given with indecent enthusiasm, of the Estates of Upper Austria. Then, after advancing to within a few leagues of Vienna, he turned north, heading for Prague. Here, too, he had a clear road, for Maria Theresa had entrusted the supreme command in Bohemia to her husband, and although the force under him was considerable, Francis hesitated and wasted time.

The Elector, his army joined by a Saxon contingent, reached Prague unopposed and stormed the city on November 26, while the Austrians stood by, a few hours' march away. On December 7 Charles Albert had himself proclaimed King of Bohemia, and the spectacle of Linz was repeated. Over 400 members of the Estates, including the representatives of the highest families, flocked to do him homage. Then, on January 24, 1742, he was elected Emperor, by all 8 votes cast at the conclave, and crowned a fortnight later, the first non-Habsburg to achieve that dignity since Sigismund of Luxemburg.[1]

But in reality, those memorable days of early September had seen the turning of the tide. Most of the Hungarian troops arrived, it is true, late, and never on the scale promised, but some contingents were soon in the

[1] Albrecht II had been elected King of the Germans in 1438, but had died before being crowned Emperor.

field, and the political effect of Hungary's decision to stand by the Queen was enormous. As for Frederick, he had rejected with scorn the suggestion that he might turn against France. 'If the Queen loses a single battle,' he had replied contemptuously, 'she will be lost beyond hope. Do you believe in an Austrian miracle?' Now, however, probably over-estimating the scale and the immediacy of Hungary's military contribution, he agreed on October 9 to the curious secret Convention of Kleinschellersdorf, under which Maria Theresa consented to allow him to take the fortress of Neisse after a sham resistance, and then to leave him unmolested there, while Frederick allowed the Austrian troops facing him to withdraw. Negotiations for a separate peace were to begin before the end of the year: under it, Austria was to cede Lower Silesia.

Frederick seems to have made this agreement out of fear of being over-reached by his allies, and he broke it, quite cold-bloodedly, after only a few weeks. But those weeks had given Maria Theresa an invaluable breathing-space, as had Charles Albert's decision, imposed on him by Belle-Isle, but seconded by his own mistrust of Saxony, to march on Prague, instead of Vienna, which he could have taken for the asking, since it was as good as undefended. But now, troops from the Silesian front were brought back to Vienna, where they were reinforced by contingents rushed up from Italy and by some Hungarians, and put, for once, under a competent commander, Count Ludwig Khevenhüller, one of the few Austrian Generals who had emerged from the Turkish War with an untarnished reputation (it was a tragedy for Austria when he died suddenly, in 1744). Small as the force was—under 16,000 in all, and not all of them regulars—Khevenhüller re-took Linz with it on January 23, 1742. Then, pressing forward, he entered Munich on February 14, so that the Elector of Bavaria lost his capital and most of his dominions only two days after being elected Emperor.

The plan of this diversion had been Maria Theresa's own, and she had, again, adhered to it against the advice of almost all her Ministers. Now that it had succeeded, she turned to the liberation of Bohemia. 'My decision is taken,' she had written to Kinsky after the fall of Prague: 'everything must be risked, to save Bohemia. All my armies, all the Hungarians must perish before I cede anything. . . . You will say that I am cruel: it is true, but I also know very well that I shall be able to make good a hundredfold all hard things that I commit in this hour to keep the Land. I shall do it, but in this hour my heart must be closed against pity.'

She could speak so with a better heart, because in these weeks an important change had come about in the international alignment. Walpole resigned in February 1742, and the conduct of Britain's foreign policy had passed into the hands of the far more bellicose Carteret, who was in favour of an 'active' policy against France. He raised Maria Theresa's subsidy to £5,000,000, persuaded King George to abandon the neutrality of Hanover, and set about organising a 'Pragmatic Army' which should give Austria active military help. But he still insisted that Maria Theresa must make peace with Frederick, who meanwhile had taken the field again, regardless of his promises. He was, however, running short of funds, and also afraid that France might make peace behind his back. He was thus susceptible to pressure, and Maria Theresa, too, decided, although with bleeding heart, that she had no course but to accept the proffered British mediation. The results of this were embodied in the Preliminary Peace of Breslau (June 11) and the definitive one of Berlin (July 28). These cost Maria Theresa all Silesia except Teschen, Troppau and Jägerndorf, and also the Moravian County of Glatz, but it freed her hands to turn against her other enemies, which were soon diminished by Saxony, which adhered to the Treaty of Berlin on September 17.

She turned with characteristic vigour. When an emissary came to her from Cardinal Fleury with overtures, she answered: 'Under the pressure of necessity, I abased my royal dignity, and wrote to the Cardinal in words which should have melted the hardest stone; he rejected my prayers.' Now she rejected his; she would not even grant terms of surrender to the French force shut up in Prague, and ordered Königsegg to break off the negotiations which Belle-Isle had begun on the question. In fact, largely owing to the sluggishness of the Austrian command—Francis being again the chief culprit—the bulk of the French succeeded in making their way out of the beleaguered city. Nevertheless, by the end of the year there were no more foreign troops on Austrian soil, and now Maria Theresa determined to carry the hostilities further afield. Her ambitions were running high; she dreamed of annulling the Imperial election, the validity of which she contested, of annexing Bavaria, perhaps compensating the Emperor in the Netherlands, even of recovering for the Empire its *avulsa*, its 'lost territories' of Alsace and Lorraine.

She had withdrawn her armies from Bavaria to help in the recovery of Bohemia, so that the Elector had been able to re-occupy his capital. But now she sent them south again, in greater force, and in June poor Charles Albert was in flight again. Meanwhile, the 'Pragmatic Army', after long sitting motionless in Holland, awaiting the accession of a Dutch contingent which never materialised, had at last taken the field, under the personal command of King George, and on June 27 won a considerable, although rather fortunate, victory over the French at Dettingen.

The victory was not followed up, and more delays

followed, but in the summer of 1744 the Austrian armies, under Francis' brother, Prince Charles of Lorraine, were actually across the Rhine. They had to withdraw, because their success brought Frederick, as unmindful of his word as ever, back into the field to re-invade Bohemia and occupy once more the luckless city of Prague; all Austria's available forces had to be mustered against this the most dangerous of all her enemies, and meanwhile, things went ill for the British, now formally at war with France, in the Netherlands. This, however, did not prevent Maria Theresa from realising one of her most cherished war-aims, at the expense, indeed, of other ambitions. The unfortunate Charles Albert returned to his capital for the third time in 1744, and died on January 20, 1745. On April 22 his boy-successor, Maximilian Joseph, concluded the Peace of Füssen, under which he was reinstated in Bavaria, but recognised the Pragmatic Sanction and promised to vote for Francis as the new Emperor. Six more votes, including Maria Theresa's own, given *qua* ruler of Bohemia, were collected, and the election duly took place on September 13, the coronation following on October 4.

Then, on December 25, the 'Second Silesian War', in which fortunes had swayed most variously, was ended by the Peace of Dresden, concluded under pressure from Britain, exercised on both parties, which re-established the *status quo* of Berlin, and thus ended the fighting in Germany. It did not end the war, for hostilities against France and Spain had been in progress in Italy since 1741. Maria Theresa promptly transferred thither the forces released from the Silesian front, and here the fighting went on for another two years, largely of her will; for under an alliance concluded between Austria, Britain and Sardinia in 1741, she had had to promise to cede to the King of Sardinia considerable territories in North Italy, (the parallelism of British policy in Sardinia and Prussia is very close), and now she had visions of compensating herself by re-conquering Naples and Sicily. But by 1745 Maria Theresa's ambitions in Italy had become only side-issues in a conflict of world-wide dimensions of which the protagonists were Britain and France, and its decisions fought out by land and sea in the Low Countries and as far afield as Canada and Madras, not to mention Scotland. The details of all this cannot find a place in a history of Austria, or a biography of Maria Theresa. This can record only the end, which came at last only in 1748, when Britain and France agreed over the Empress' head. Left alone, she was forced, on October 23, to accede to the Treaty of Aix-la-Chapelle. Under this she lost not only the territories which Charles Emmanuel had made his price, but also Parma, Piacenza, and Guastalla, ceded to the Infante of Spain. She received, indeed, the Powers' guarantee of her remaining possessions, but that guarantee applied also to Frederick's acquisitions in Silesia. Russia, it is true, had gone a little further, for in June, 1746, she had signed with Austria a secret Treaty of Mutual Defence which contained a special provision that Austria should be entitled to re-occupy Silesia and Glatz if Prussia attacked Austria, Poland or Russia.

II

On the face of them, the Treaties of Dresden and Aix-la-Chapelle were poor reward for seven years of exhausting struggle, and it is easy to understand Maria Theresa's lack of resignation to them, and especially her wrath with Britain, who egged her on to fight France when it suited her, and when her interests required it, imposed on her sacrifice after sacrifice, often over her head. 'Why,' she asked Robinson, when the Franco-British conversations were going on at Aix, 'am I excluded from negotiations which concern my own affairs? My enemies will give me better conditions than my friends. . . . Your King of Sardinia gets everything, not the slightest consideration is paid to me. And on top of it, there is your King of Prussia, as well.'

Silesia was certainly a heavy loss from every point of view. The effect on the balance of power in Germany of its transference from Austrian to Prussian sovereignty was enormous, perhaps decisive for the whole future. The economic blow to Austria was very heavy, since Silesia had been, industrially, the most advanced Province of the whole central Monarchy. Another shift, the importance of which appeared only later, was in the power-position between Germans and Slavs in the Monarchy in general and the Bohemian Lands in particular. But the balance-sheet of the years must take into account not only what was lost, but what was snatched from the very brink of perdition, and by comparison with what its enemies had intended, and all but achieved in 1741, the condition in which the 'House of Austria' emerged in 1747 was well-nigh miraculous. The great bulk of its territories were, after all, still intact. It had recovered the Imperial Crown. It stood an undisputed Great Power, and for another 150 years there was to be no more talk of dismembering it.

And this was very largely Maria Theresa's personal achievement. Alone, she had stood firm when all around her counselled yielding to the Prussian. Alone, she had changed the hearts of the Hungarians. 'I am only a woman,' she had said in the dark days at Pozsony, 'but I have the heart of a king.' She had proved it.

She had done much more than save her crown, for the internal consolidation which had taken place after the crisis had been phenomenal. No more danger had threatened from Hungary, and in the West, as soon as the wind changed, the Bohemian and Upper Austrian Estates had fallen over themselves to explain away their defection and protest their devotion. Maria Theresa had, most naturally, been deeply incensed against the Bohemian nobles, most of whom, as she commented bitterly, owed their titles and their estates to the munificence of her ancestors.[1] At first, she proposed to mete out appropriate justice. She set up a Commission which divided offenders into the real traitors, the 'searchers after novelty' and those who had erred 'out of light-mindedness', and condign proceedings were instituted against the first category. It would, however, have been impossible to proceed with full rigour without making something like a clean sweep of the class, for there was hardly a noble family of which at least one member had not offended; the Commission itself was composed of men who, if their own records were clear, had brothers or cousins who were compromised. It trod most warily, admitting extenuating circumstances wherever this was at all possible. And Maria Theresa herself, peppery as she was, was quite remarkably unvindictive—in all her life, there were only two persons whom she never forgave, one, Frederick of Prussia, the other, an officer who advised her husband to occupy a separate bedroom as the means of bringing her to heel when she was refractory.

In the end, the peccant nobles got off lightly enough. Some who were foreign subjects had their estates confiscated. Of the natives, one was sentenced to death *in absentia*, a few were fined, and a few more lost their patents of nobility. Maria Theresa was harder on some peasants who had taken up arms for Charles Albert against promises of freedom. Their villages were razed to the ground, and a really savage sentence pronounced

[1] The Bohemian nobility was largely composed of the descendants of soldiers of fortune on whom Ferdinand II had bestowed the estates confiscated from the Protestant rebels after the Battle of the White Mountain in 1620.

(although not executed) on a young burgher of Prague who had distributed leaflets inciting them to revolt. Another body to suffer badly was the old-established Jewish community of Prague, which had followed the example of its superiors in welcoming the foreigner. Maria Theresa, who always detested Jews, wanted to expel them altogether, and had begun the process when the urgent representations of the Estates moved her to call it off. But they were subjected to a swingeing fine (the ghetto was also thoroughly plundered afterwards by the wild Croat irregular pandurs).

When Maria Theresa went to Prague in 1743 to be crowned, she started off in ill-humour, but the ceremony ended in prolonged and gay festivities, as though nothing had ever been wrong. The Estates of Upper Austria got off more lightly still: a sponge was passed over the whole affair.

Her clemency was rewarded: thereafter her throne was as secure at home as abroad, and her authority unquestioned. No one in Bohemia took Frederick's side in 1744 and 1745.

Meanwhile, her own life had not been all drab. It had had its great moments, the highest of all—probably for her personally, the peak of her life—the occasion when her husband was crowned Emperor. She was not crowned with him: he had wished it, but she declined on various pretexts; one, that she was in her then customary condition—in fact, in the eighth month of pregnancy. Another pretext, which may have been a real consideration, was shortage of funds: an Imperial coronation was by tradition an occasion of the utmost pomp, at which the assembled sovereigns vied with one another in display, and if Maria Theresa participated in it officially, she could not do it on the cheap: it was calculated that the pleasure would cost her three million gulden. Some historians believe her real motive to have been a feeling that the empty prestige of the Imperial Crown would dim the radiance of the two which she already wore in her own right. At any rate, she gave up the thought: the 'Great Empress' was never an Empress crowned. She came to Frankfurt, but as a private person and watched the proceedings from the window of a private house. It is true that her charm and her *bruyant* acclamation of her husband as he paced below her in the procession made her, as Goethe, who describes the event, recorded, the most popular figure of the whole spectacle.

Nor was this an isolated pleasure. The word 'festivities', used on an earlier page, may have read oddly, but the coronation in Prague took place at a stage of the war when Austrian territory was clear of foreign enemies, and the campaigns still in process were being fought on foreign soil, largely with hired foreign troops, in an atmosphere which presaged victory. Even the Second Silesian War lacked the desperate urgency of the First. And in general, these years which followed the banishment of the extreme danger to her throne were probably the happiest of Maria Theresa's life, certainly the gayest. All the natural high spirits which had found insufficient vent during her somewhat secluded childhood, came bubbling out now. She was still young, still agile and graceful, in love and beloved, widely popular by now, especially among her own Viennese, a figure abroad, and in the mood to enjoy her triumphs. She had, it is true, dutifully cut her Court expenditure and replaced her father's grandiose Spanish ceremonial by more homely ways; the holders of many sinecures had lost them (these included the 'Spanish leeches') and such extravagances as Charles' £30,000 theatrical performance were no more. But she left herself enough for enjoyment. The climax of the whole was a grand 'carrousel', held on January 2, 1743, to celebrate the liberation of Prague. It had been three months in the preparing, and took the form of a tourney between four teams of women, two on horseback, two in chariots, held in the Spanish Riding Academy. Maria Theresa herself, seated side-saddle, on account of her almost habitual condition, conducted the proceedings and afterwards led the teams through the streets of Vienna.

The carnival saw a plethora of *bals masqués*, after some of which the Queen and her consort, with a few attendants, visited in disguise the popular Viennese dance-hall, the *Mehlgrube*. She was inexhaustible: she was able to dance all night, and to sit down to her papers in the morning, after having attended Divine Service. There were concerts, operas, theatres, of all of which Maria Theresa, although by no means such a virtuoso as her father, was yet an enthusiastic patroness. There were excursions on horseback, for having once learnt to ride, Maria Theresa took to the pastime enthusiastically, especially since it enabled her to gratify her passion for fresh air. There was also play, to which both she and her husband were strongly addicted. She established a faro bank in the *retirada*, her private apartments, and would spend whole nights at the card table. The stakes were often very high: Francis once lost 30,000 ducats at a sitting. But, fortunately perhaps for the State finances, Maria Theresa's own luck was proverbial. She often, indeed, renounced her winnings when they could have put her partners in difficulty.

Another joy was the marriage, in January, 1744, of her beloved sister Marianne to her hardly less dear brother-in-law, Charles of Lorraine. This, indeed, was short-lived; Marianne died in December of the same year, after being delivered of a still-born child.

*   *   *

This will be the place to mention one figure who played a most curious, indeed, a unique part in Maria Theresa's life. This was Count (later Prince) Emanuel Silva

Tarouca, a gentleman of Portuguese origin who had entered the Austrian service as a young man and had risen to a high post in the Netherlands Council. In December, 1740, Maria Theresa had both promoted him President of the Council, and given him the commission of waiting on her daily, not only to report on the affairs of his Department but also to advise her on intimate and family business. A few months later, she conferred on him the extraordinary commission of watching over her personal behaviour and giving her frank and unsparing advice on it. It may be said that he carried out this strange duty scrupulously for many years, while she took his admonitions, which were sometimes severe, in unfailing good part, and in her *Political Testament* pays him the warmest of tributes of gratitude, respect and affection.

III

Meanwhile, she had signed the Treaties, first of Dresden, then of Aix-la-Chapelle, only *à contrecoeur*, and without any intention of accepting them as final: for this, both the intrinsic magnitude of her loss, and the perfidious manner in which it had been inflicted on her, had been far too great. Consequently, if the years which followed were years of peace, it was, essentially, a peace which, to adapt Clausewitz' words, was a continuation of war by other methods. These resulted, indeed, in a series of reforms many of which were far too radical to be described as mere preparations for offensive war, or even for defence, and it would even be unfair to ignore the operation of other considerations in many of them; but it would be equally mistaken to overlook Maria Theresa's final, over-riding purpose behind them all, which was to strengthen and consolidate her State as a military machine.

These years—those of her 'First Reform Period' in

which, suddenly throwing aside her youthful gaiety, she transformed herself into an austere and tireless dictator— are far from being the most picturesque of her life, but if we except 1741, they are probably the most important and productive, to be compared only with her second and rather similar spurt of activity after her husband's death, and surpassing that in vigour and originality, although not, perhaps, in depth.

During the war years, Maria Theresa had already made a few changes among her official advisers. Shortly after her accession, she had taken Count Philip Kinsky, the 'Supreme Chancellor' of Bohemia, into the Privy Conference. When Sinzendorf died in 1742, she had promoted his former second in command for foreign affairs, Uhlfeld, to his portfolio and seat. When Alois Harrach died, later in the same year, she had taken in two more new men: her old Master of the Household, Count Leopold Herberstein (whose previous post was given to Count Johann Khevenhüller[1]), and Alois Harrach's son, Friedrich. Later vacancies were filled by Count Rudolph Colloredo, former Imperial Vice-Chancellor, and Salburg, head of the War Commissariat. There had also been certain changes in the machinery of government. When Uhlfeld was promoted, his portfolio was taken from the Austrian Court Chancellery and made into the *Haus- und Hof-Kanzlei* (Dynastic and Court Chancellery[2]). The financial and military systems had been simplified by the abolition, as a superfluous complication, of the Finance Conference and the sub-war offices in Graz and Innsbruck. The control of mines

[1] Author of the voluminous diary which forms a major source for the intimate history of the Austrian Court over thirty years. He was appointed to the Conference in 1748.

[2] The new Ministry took over diplomatic relations with Russia; those with the Porte remained in charge of the War Council until 1753.

and the mint had been taken from the Camera. A new organisation (to which we shall return) had been set up for the promotion of trade and industry. The Austrian Court Chancellery had further ceded its function of Supreme Court of Appeal to a commission appointed to clear up its arrears of work. The War Council was re-organised in 1745 and the War Commissariat promoted to the rank of an independent Ministry in 1746. The administration of the Bánát and the Military Frontier was reorganised.

Some of these administrative changes proved in the event to be important. The appointment of the judicial commission, meant at the time to be a temporary measure, proved the first step towards the later separation of the judiciary from the administrative system, and the independent Ministry of Foreign Affairs was an important innovation. It also gave Maria Theresa personally a far greater voice in foreign policy, for Uhlfeld, who was in any case no genius, could not dictate to her as Sinzen-dorf had done. It was reserved for Kaunitz, when he succeeded to the post in 1753, to make it the key one in the Monarchy; from 1742 to 1753 Maria Theresa was in practice her own Foreign Minister, as, for that matter, she (with her husband) had from the first taken the top-level decisions on military policy.

Most of these moves, however, had been simple *ad hoc* adjustments to meet special situations. Few of them had done much to raise the intellectual level of the government of the Monarchy. Only Friedrich Harrach, who had been put on the Conference as a consolation prize for not getting the Chancellorship which he had expected, (allegedly, Bartenstein had got it given to Uhlfeld, as easier for himself to control), was, by general consent, an extremely able man. But Herberstein, although honest, was politically a null: he had been given the post only because he made himself intolerably disagreeable until he got it. Khevenhüller was solely interested in questions of Court protocol.

Neither had any of the changes remedied the central weaknesses of the general system, as Maria Theresa had inherited it: the inability of the Crown to impose its will on the selfish and mutually jealous Provincial 'capi', and to extract from them the resources which it needed for its own purposes. Friedrich Harrach, for all his ability, proved himself, when appointed Supreme Chancellor of Bohemia in 1745[1] and when acting 'Provincial Marshal' of Lower Austria,[2] the very personification of class and provincial interests. Kinsky was the worst of the lot. Maria Theresa, who then entertained a certain personal affection for him, had taken him into the Conference to stop his complaints that the 'Austrian' Provinces were over-represented there at the expense of the Bohemian; but no sooner arrived, he set the whole body by the ears by his intemperate championship of the provincial interests of Bohemia. It was, indeed, he who had been largely responsible for the whole original catastrophe. The choice of a General to meet Frederick had lain between Neipperg and Khevenhüller, but the latter had stipulated for a sizeable force and guarantees that it would be paid regularly. The direct cost of supplying the army would have fallen on the Bohemian Provinces, and Kinsky had shouted so loudly that this could not be done without 'ruining the Provinces' that Maria Theresa, in 'a well-meant attempt to establish good harmony between the Generals Commanding and the Supreme Chancellor, who had to supply the armies', had opted instead for Neipperg, whose demands had been more modest, and as it proved, fatally insufficient.

[1] In that year Kinsky, whose health was failing, had been moved to a financial position.

[2] He was holding this position temporarily, *vice* his brother Ferdinand, who had been sent down to Milan.

Maria Theresa must have become increasingly alive, as the years passed, to the basic weaknesses of the political 'system,' but preoccupied as she was with questions of high foreign and military policy, she had not gone deeply into their causes. It was, by her own confession, only when 'she saw that she must put her hand to the Peace of Dresden' that she acquired a new angle of vision. The words in which she expresses herself in this famous passage in her *Political Testament* are not quite lucid, for in them she mingles two sets of deductions from her central, and imperfectly stated, premise; but the sense of them is that she now felt internal consolidation to be the Monarchy's chief need, so urgent and so imperative that it was more important to get down to it quickly than to prolong the war, even if this meant sacrificing the Netherlands or Italy. From that moment on, she writes, she devoted her whole attention to informing herself of 'the situation and strength of the Provinces' and to acquiring a clear picture of the weaknesses and abuses which had crept into their systems.

Her 'Ministers', themselves the authors and beneficiaries of the evils, naturally would not help her in these enquiries—as the Prussian envoy to her Court observed, they were at pains to hide the truth from her. But by now she had acquired her own helpers and confidants: besides her husband and, chiefly in another field, Silva Tarouca, she had Bartenstein, to whom she had become reconciled, and her private secretary, Ignaz Koch, described by her in her *Testament* as 'a man of unexampled discretion, and also uncommonly Christian and free from intrigue.' Chiefly thanks to these two men, who brought her 'secret information', she was able, in a year or so, to form a fair enough picture of the situation. She would, however, still have found it difficult to put through her will against her Ministers, and she hesitated to dismiss them, partly out of fear of provoking more opposition from them and their allies than she yet cared to face, and partly, by her own testimony, out of a feeling that it would be contrary to the family tradition, for which she retained throughout her life a curiously deep reverence, to dismiss honest servants of long standing. She might have delayed many years before venturing on the reforms now to be described if, as she writes frankly, 'God himself had not drawn a line by letting all the old men die off.' This line was reasonably complete by the end of 1745, for after Sinzendorf and Alois Harrach in 1742, Herberstein had died in 1744 and Starhemberg in 1745, by which time Kinsky and Königsegg were more or less out of action, leaving, of the original team, only Joseph Harrach immovably entrenched in his post, whence he could not be evicted until 1762 (he died in 1764). And now, she writes, a man 'was truly sent me by Providence, for to break through, I had to have such a man, honourable, disinterested, unprejudiced, without personal ambition or convictions, who supported the good because he recognised it for such.' This man was Count Friedrich Wilhelm Haugwitz, one of the most important figures of all her reign.

The son of a General in the Saxon service, Haugwitz as a young man had adopted Catholicism and entered the Austrian service, rising to a respectable position in the Provincial administration of Silesia. When Frederick occupied the Province, he had left it to come to Vienna, where he arrived almost penniless. Her attention drawn to him, Maria Theresa had put him in charge of the administration of the rump Province, and soon found him to be indeed the man whom she needed. Owing to his origin, he was uncorrupted by personal or family interest; he was fabulously hardworking and mentally fearless; and he held, out of conviction, acquired through considerable reading, the tenet that the true form of State was that of benevolent despotism and that the function of administration was to provide the Prince with the money to maintain his rule and to promote the welfare of his subjects. These objects could be achieved only if political and financial control were vested in the same hands—translated into terms of practice, if all taxation was levied by the State. In his new post (where special conditions made this possible) he put his theories into practice with such effect as nearly to double the revenue from the Province. Then in 1743 he sent Maria Theresa a detailed blue-print for the application of his system in the Province as a whole, when it should have been recovered, supporting his proposals by drawing a contrast between the inefficiencies of the Austrian system and the successful methods, which he had studied carefully, used by Frederick across the frontier.

Silesia as a whole was, of course, not recovered, but Maria Theresa allowed Haugwitz to consolidate his little dictatorship in the rump Province, where the whole tax services were transferred to the State in 1744, the Estates being left with only their judicial functions. Then, in 1747, she sent him down as Commissioner to Carniola and Carinthia, both of which had fallen heavily in arrears with their *contributio*. Haugwitz dealt with this situation by an operation which amounted, in effect, to putting in State bailiffs in the form of State 'Representations', in charge of 'all Cameral, commercial and administrative questions, without exception.' Maria Theresa backed him to the full. When the Estates of Carniola complained that the new *contributio* required of them was too high, they were told that 'the Crown expressly commands them to grant these sums voluntarily.' In Carinthia all payments were cut off until the consent was given.

The next development was on the grand scale. As with many of the important moves of Maria Theresa's reign, we are tantalisingly ignorant of the pre-history of this one, but about June 1747, when peace with France seemed to be on the threshold, Maria Theresa accepted an estimate from her advisers that for future military purposes, which would not include balance of power wars against France, the Monarchy would need a standing army of 108,000 men, not including the Military Frontier levies or the forces from Hungary, the Netherlands or the Milanese.[1]

The upkeep of this force would require 14 million gulden a year. When none of the Ministers could suggest how this sum could be raised, Maria Theresa asked Haugwitz to submit proposals. His plan was simple, although it involved a large breach with tradition. The Provinces were to raise the increased sums primarily by the extension of the land tax to the previously tax-free demesne lands of the nobles (the payment was, indeed, to be at a lighter rate than that levied on the peasants' lands). In return, the Estates were to be relieved of or refunded all expenditure connected with the quartering, supply, etc., of the troops stationed in them (this would now fall exclusively on the War Commissariat) and they were to get an alleviation in respect of their debts: of the 5 per cent paid by them only 4 per cent would be treated as interest, while 1 per cent would go towards amortisation.

The money would still be voted by the Estates, now, as a fixed and general rule, every ten years, for the decade in advance. It was to be collected monthly, through the Estates, but thereafter became the property of the State.

These proposals did not go unopposed. Maria Theresa first had them shown to Friedrich Harrach, who, while not denying the necessity of raising the sum indicated, produced a plan which, from the political point of view,

[1] These were calculated at 24,000 from the Frontier, 26,000 from the Milanese, 24,000 from the Netherlands and 20–30,000 from the Hungarian *insurrectio*.

was the exact opposite of Haugwitz'. Instead of the *contributio* being turned, in practice, into a State service, the Cameral and other State resources were to be transferred to the Estates, which were then to be left free to choose their own way of raising the sum. But Maria Theresa had made up her mind. On January 29, 1748, she submitted the whole question to a Crown Council. At this, in reality, hardly any of its participants supported Haugwitz' plan (her own account of the meeting is quite misleading). Nevertheless, she announced that she was adopting it, signing the minutes with the bitter comment:

'*Placet*, and it is only too true that this is a correct record. In fifty years' time no one will believe that these were my Ministers, who were created by me.'

Haugwitz was told to get on with the next step, which was to get the consent of the Provincial Estates for this diminution of their privileges and partial abrogation of their rights. This proved, in the event, unexpectedly easy in the first two Provinces approached by him, Moravia and Bohemia: they may have been cowed by recent memories, and the exchange of obligations was not a bad bargain for Provinces so frequently theatres of war as they had been. In some other Provinces the resistance was stiffer, but Maria Theresa simply over-ruled opposition with a high hand, and by the autumn, all the Provinces had agreed to the higher figure, and nearly all of them, to the ten-years rule (the Tirol was allowed to keep the annual vote, and some other Provinces received smaller concessions).

In each Province, meanwhile, there had been established 'Deputations', corresponding to the 'Representations' previously installed by Haugwitz in Silesia, Carinthia and Carniola, and in charge of all *militaria mixta, contributionalia and cameralia* (i.e. all financial business, including the upkeep of the army). These bodies were made equal in status to the Provincial

Estates, which therefore could not intervene in their
operations, and they reported directly to a central 'Chief
Deputation', which sat in Vienna, under the Presidency
of the Monarch herself. 'Chambers', again one for each
Province, constituted Courts of Appeal for the local
judicatures. Since the terms of reference of the Deputations and Chambers covered all the most important
questions previously handled by the Estates, the importance of the latter was reduced at one blow by some
90 per cent. Simultaneously, another, most important,
change was introduced on the next level down: the *Kreis*
(Circle) offices which had previously been maintained in
Bohemia as local agencies of the Estates, and controlled
by them, were made State organs under the Deputations
and similar offices set up in the other larger Provinces.

Next the financial system was reorganised. The Camera, as an independent service, was reduced to its Hungarian, Tirolean and Vorlande branches; the revenues
from these went to the service of the debt (which was
dealt with by a special department, of which Francis
himself took charge) and the expenditure of the Court and
central administration. All its other organisations were
put under the Central and Provincial Deputations and
their receipts merged with those coming in to the
Deputations from the *contributio*.

The final step, which Maria Theresa herself probably
thought the most important of all, and which most likely
—although here, again, the documents fail us—was
taken on her personal insistence, came a year later: she
seems to have thought it wiser not to take it until peace was
concluded and the troops back in their stations. On
May 2, 1749, the Bohemian and Austrian Court Chancelleries were abolished, as was the now superfluous
'Head Deputation', and two great organisations set up
in their places: the *Directorium in Publicis et Cam-*
eralibus (Directorate of Administration and Finance) of

which Haugwitz became President, for all administrative and financial questions, and an *Oberste Justizstelle* (Supreme Judiciary) which combined the functions of Ministry of Justice and Supreme Court of Appeal. The competence of each of these extended to the whole of both groups of Provinces, which retained, indeed, their individual entities under them; every measure enacted centrally was transmitted to each Province separately, even when its wording was the same in each case, while reasonable allowance was often made for local conditions.

To placate Harrach, a *Konferenz in Internis* (Conference for Internal Business), under his Presidency, was set up, nominally as the supreme organ of control of the whole structure, but in fact, it exercised no influence and when, a month later, Harrach died (of smallpox) it faded out of existence.

The whole of the German-Austrian and Bohemian Provinces were now covered with a net-work of State instances, all subordinated to a single centre and controlling almost every aspect of public life above the manorial level and that of the local urban autonomies. The change, moreover, meant much more than a simple transference of functions from one set of hands to another, for as time went on, the 'Representations' and their successors, and the Circles, not only took over from the Estates one after another of the activities originally left them, but also engaged in many more. The Circles, in particular, whose chief original functions had been to carry out the tasks previously performed by the Estates in connection with the local troops—quartering, purchase of supplies, etc.—soon became responsible for communications, public health, security, prisons, weights and measures, control of markets, forestry services, and a host of other questions many of which had not previously been subject to official control at all.

It was, furthermore, true only in one sense that their

competence ceased at the level described. Maria Theresa did not abolish the old self-governing town and village institutions, nor the manorial system as such—at this stage of her life she thought this neither practically feasible, nor even right in principle. 'Entirely to abolish villeinage,' she had written in 1742, 'can never be regarded as practicable, since there is no country which makes no difference between lord and subject; to free the peasant from his duty to the former would make the one unbridled and the other discontented, and would, in general, be an infringement of justice.' But although (contrary to mythos) her social sense was by no means hypertrophied, either now or later, she was not blind to what Haugwitz, in a favourite phrase of his, called 'the equality which is pleasing to God', and still less, to the practical consideration that if the peasant was overburdened by his landlord's demands, he would be unable to meet those of the State. One of the chief duties laid on the Circle officers was to see that the taxes came in, and for that the peasants had to be *steuerfähig*—in a condition to pay what was demanded of them. The officers were therefore instructed, as a major part of their duties, to protect the peasants against illegal exactions by their lords and to see that the Estates as a whole did not spare their members' own lands at the cost of the peasants'. Conversion of peasant-land to demesne was prohibited strictly; even if a peasant was evicted from his holding, or it became vacant for any other reason, it had to be assigned to another peasant cultivator. All important disputes between lords and peasants had to be referred to authority, and where it was found that a peasant had been over-reached or oppressed by the manorial lord, or his agent, the victim was to be compensated and the culprit punished.

In certain local cases, the maximum level of dues and services was laid down. This was, so far, usually done *ad hoc*, where doubt had arisen as to the legal situation in some particular locality, but in one area, the small and remote one of Slavonia, which had never been properly surveyed nor the law in it fixed beyond doubt, a survey was carried through and an *Urbarium* issued which laid down the size of a plot deemed to constitute a peasant holding, and the rent in cash, kind and services attaching to it.

* * *

What is true of so many of Maria Theresa's reforms must be said also of those of 1748 and 1749. They were severely pragmatic, undertaken with the object of increasing efficiency, and above all, the financial resources of the State, and they did not go beyond what was necessary for the purpose. They did not even entail a dethronement of the aristocracy, as a class: the top offices remained reserved for the members of the great families, and it was quite exceptional for an untitled man to be appointed even Circle Commissioner. They did, however, transform the holders of these offices from servants of their Provinces and their classes into those of the State, and this was an enormous change, the most important internal development of Maria Theresa's reign. They also proved enduring. Some features of them were, as will be seen, modified subsequently: in particular, the question whether administration and finance should be handled on the top level by one Ministry, or by two (or even more), was reconsidered repeatedly. The central principles, however, were never revoked. In the Provinces in which the reforms applied, the substitution of bureaucratic control for self-government remained a permanency. The Estates never recovered even one iota of the powers now taken away from them; on the contrary, the whole trend was thereafter further to whittle away all self-government down to the communal level. Similarly, as between central and local government, the trend was regularly in favour of the former. Finally, the administrative and judicial unification, on the top level, of the German-Austrian and Bohemian groups of Provinces remained intact until 1848, and the political unification of them, as a single Parliamentary entity, disappeared only in 1918. In this sense, the reform of 1749 was the progenitor of the political quasi-entity which formed the partner to Hungary under the 'Dualist System' established in 1867.

The changes further represented a prolongation, and in some respects an accentuation, of the official distinction between the German and Bohemian Provinces on the one hand, and on the other, the rest of the Monarchy, to which they were not extended. The Netherlands and the Italian Provinces were in any case so remote that they could not be fitted into any general pattern. Their separate Councils were demoted to sections of the Court Chancellery, but these, at least that for the Netherlands, remained mere post-boxes. As to Hungary, Maria Theresa herself recognised that it would have been impossible to impose the changes in the way she had done in the West: they would have to be negotiated with a legally convoked Diet, and this would have been highly unlikely to accept taxation on noble land only eight years after its exemption therefrom had been elevated to the status of an 'eternal and immutable fundamental law'. It would also presumably have seized the occasion of its convocation to present all manner of *gravamina* to which Maria Theresa did not want to listen.

Financial stringency nevertheless compelled her to convoke a Diet in 1751, but warned by her Hungarian advisers, she did not even suggest extending the Haugwitz reforms to Hungary: she asked the Diet only for an increase in the *contributio* from the 2,500,000 gulden which had been traditional in Charles' day, to 3,700,000. Even so, the occasion proved a disappointment to both sides. The Diet produced a list of 122 *gravamina*, offering to pay a *contributio* of 2,750,000 gulden if they were remedied. With great difficulty it was induced to raise its offer to 3,200,000, in return for a few, very minor, concessions. Queen and nation parted in mutual ill-humour. 'My very name has been reviled,' Maria Theresa wrote in her message to the Diet. 'Sorrow fills my heart as I see the Estates treat me in a manner never heretofore experienced by any of their kings.' And she adjured them 'to desist from your mistrust towards your King, your mother, so that you recover the grace and favour which you have lost.'

So Hungary remained exempt from taxation on its nobles' lands, nor were the rest of the Haugwitz reforms extended to the country. The Hungarian Court Chancellery was not merged in the Directorate, its Supreme Court remained independent, and perhaps most important of all, its local units, the Counties, remained autonomous units in the hands of elected representatives of the local nobles; no Circle officials took over, or even supervised, their doings. The resultant dualism between 'Austria' and Hungary was consequently not only political, but also fiscal, administrative, and in its further consequences, social and, as will be seen, economic also.

* * *

The reorganisation of the military forces was commenced as soon as that of the administrative system had gone far enough to make this possible. On February 8, 1748, thus less than a fortnight after the historic meeting at which she had accepted Haugwitz' proposals—she was wasting no time at this stage in her career—Maria Theresa appointed a Committee to consider the problem. Its terms of reference were complementary to those given to Haugwitz: how to make 108,000 men (excluding the subsidiary forces) into an efficient force on a budget of 14 million gulden. As President of the Committee she appointed her brother-in-law, Prince Charles, but the planner in chief was Feldzeugmeister Daun, a son-in-law of 'die Füchsin' and a personal favourite of Maria Theresa.

Daun was destined later to prove himself only a degree less of a failure in the field than Prince Charles himself. A master of tactics, he was yet of so hesitant and cautious a disposition as time and again to allow Frederick, who understood mobility, to retrieve situations which ought to have been hopeless. But he was a good organiser, and now carried through many useful reforms. The War Council itself was reorganised, a new manual of infantry training, modelled on the Prussian, introduced, making drill, tactical training, etc., uniform in all units, and the infantry given new muskets, again copied from the Prussian. The artillery and engineers were reorganised similarly. A system of large-scale manoeuvres was introduced.

Maria Theresa took a lively personal interest in this work. She often visited the camps and attended the manoeuvres on horse-back; a commemorative medal struck during these years bore her portrait with the legend *mater castrorum* ('Mother of the Camps'). She personally founded a military academy (in Wiener Neustadt), a training college for engineers (in Vienna) and a cadet school at which 100 sons of poor nobles or of officers could receive pre-training, passing on to the academy if they did well. To raise the social status of the corps of officers she decreed that any officer wearing uniform should rank as *hoffähig*, entitled to present himself at Court. The pay of both officers and men was improved, and they received it regularly.

The results of all this were not inconsiderable, although the complete programme of full separation of the military system from the political could not be realised, since it proved impossible to raise the figure of 108,000 by voluntary enlistment. The Estates had, after all, to be asked to supply contingents, which they did reluctantly, usually by shanghaiing unwanted elements and demanding a capitation fee, to be deducted from the *contributio*, for each man supplied. For economy's sake, and to escape wrangles with the Estates, as sparing a use as possible was made of this expedient, and the units were consequently often under strength.

* * *

All her life, Maria Theresa had a remarkably sound appreciation of the importance of the economic factor. The prevalent economic philosophy of her day, which she followed in her pragmatic fashion, was the mercantilist, and from the outset of her reign, she showed herself alive to the importance of developing the non-agricultural resources of her dominions—a need the urgency of which was increased by the loss of Silesia. 'The longer I think of it,' she wrote to Uhlfeld as early as 1743, 'the better I see that in these Provinces no sufficient attention is paid to commerce and manufactures, whereas these are the only means of helping the Lands and bringing foreign money into them.' These words accompanied an instruction to the Chancellor to resuscitate the only organisations then existing in the Monarchy which were specifically concerned with economic development, a series of *Kommerzkollegien* (Economic Committees[1]) which Charles had established in the Provincial centres. These had fallen into hibernation, from which Uhlfeld does not seem to have succeeded in rousing them, but a new

[1] In the terminology of the day the word 'commerce' covered industry in so far as it worked for a wider market. Small-scale handicrafts were known as *Polizeigewerbe* and came under the charge of the local administrative authorities.

Universalkommerzdirektorium (Directorate General of Economic Affairs), established in 1746 to deal with the whole Monarchy, with very wide terms of reference, including reform of the tariff system, expansion of communications, regulation of imports and exports, and conclusion of commercial treaties, while it failed to produce any 'universal' results, did give birth to a number of Provincial organisations, of which the Bohemian was the most vigorous.

It was also the most important, for many factors made Bohemia the obvious replacement for Silesia: similarity of natural resources and conditions, proximity (in some cases, whole enterprises moved across the frontier, workers and all) and also a labour-force more abundant and cheaper than could be found in German Austria (many of the new enterprises were worked with the *robot*, the peasant's due in labour). The director of the organisation, Count Hatzfeld (the later Minister of State), was an able and energetic man, and he received valuable help from Francis, who, having himself founded certain industries, toured the Province persuading its nobles to follow his example. In fact, as one authority has written, 'incomparably more was done in barely three years for the trade in linen, the woollen and cotton industry, and glass refining, than in decades previously[1].'

Progress was less rapid outside Bohemia, but both in Moravia and in the German-Austrian Provinces, especially Lower Austria, a considerable amount of industrialisation took place. The State did not usually itself act as entrepreneur, although it sometimes took over bankrupt concerns; but private entrepreneurs were encouraged and supported by facilities of all kinds, subsidies, cash advances, exemption of them from guild restrictions (although in 1752 it was decided that the

[1] G. Otruba, *Die Wirtschaftspolitik Maria Theresias* (Vienna 1963), p. 12.

guilds could not be abolished altogether) and tariff protection. Both entrepreneurs and skilled workers were not infrequently imported from abroad, the latter including men in possession of trade secrets; in what is known today as industrial espionage, Maria Theresa showed herself as personally unscrupulous as any modern American firm.

It should be emphasised that this activity, while partly the product of general considerations, was deliberately directed into the service of the cold war against Prussia which was also the dominating motive of the administrative reorganisation. While all countries wishing to trade with Austria felt the impact of it in greater or less degree —England, her ally, not least—it was most specifically directed against Prussia. This appeared partly in efforts made to direct the economic life of the Monarchy away from Prussia by enlarging the port of Trieste and finding new outlets for exports in Russia and Turkey; partly in tariff policy. The Monarchy's tariffs had previously been generally low, averaging no more than 2–3 per cent, and levied only for fiscal purposes. Now there was for some time no general increase, although high tariffs, or import prohibitions, were applied in particular cases where some new or weak industry required protection: for example, in 1749 the importation of foreign fine cloths, dresses and fancy goods was prohibited. Then, however, general high protective tariffs, averaging 30 per cent, were introduced, for the Bohemian Lands (which had meanwhile been made into a customs union) in 1751, for Hungary in 1754, and for the Archduchy of Austria and Inner Austria in 1755. The hardly concealed object of these was to ruin Prussian Silesia economically, on the calculation that the connection with the Monarchy was vital to Silesia. Frederick replied with a 30 per cent duty on Austrian paper, iron wares and tallow. Each side added further items, and now a regular tariff war was on, which was accompanied by a less embittered war with Saxony.

The second noteworthy feature of the policy of industrialisation—one which had far-reaching consequences for the history of the Monarchy, not only during Maria Theresa's reign, but long after it—was its restrictive and even actively repressive application towards Hungary. When the plans were first considered, a broad division of roles was adopted: the industries were to be in the West, while Hungary was to supply raw materials and agricultural produce. This was natural enough, for, apart from the special reasons for concentrating the first industrialisation in Bohemia, the natural facilities, the trained or trainable workers and the big markets, were all in the West; Hungary, with its undeveloped resources, its sparse and backward populations and its appalling communications, was no natural field for speedy industrialisation, and speed was what Maria Theresa wanted. It implied no discrimination against Hungary, against which Maria Theresa always set her face, and indeed, she had at this juncture much more reason to feel grateful to Hungary than she had to the Bohemian magnates; it was not meant to be permanent, nor to exclude the development of those Hungarian industries for which the natural conditions were favourable, and it was to be accompanied by measures for promoting Hungarian agriculture and above all, the country's chief need, finding outlets for its produce; the search for new commercial relations with the East was largely for Hungary's benefit.

But the atmosphere soon changed. The 'Universal' Directorate failed to produce results; it was replaced in 1749 by a new 'Directorate of Commerce' competent only for the West, and this in turn was presently swallowed up by Haugwitz' great super-Ministry. By this time the new industries were growing up and acquiring vested interests, which were directly represented in the Directorate, which was, indeed, practically the mouthpiece of the Bohemian industrialists. They now began to argue that their factories would be unable to stand up against any competition from Hungary, with the advantage enjoyed by its nobles of freedom from taxation. While the full pressure did not develop until Maria Theresa's 'Second Reform Period' (when we shall revert to the subject), the beginnings of it go back to these earlier years, during which, moreover, Hungary suffered considerably from the effects of the new tariffs and their consequences, which on the one hand hit many of her exports heavily (Silesia had been the biggest market for Hungarian wines) and on the other, made it almost impossible for her in import any manufactured goods except the expensive, and often inferior, products of the new Austrian factories. The Hungarians resented this policy acutely, and it probably did more than any other single factor to prevent political relations between Maria Theresa and Hungary from ever becoming truly cordial.

* * *

The important cultural reforms of the period were, again, severely pragmatic, and it is not unfair to describe their principle as that of mercantilism applied in the intellectual sphere. The great new foundations of the period, the State Archive, the military academies, the 'Oriental Academy', which was originally set up to train native dragomans and interpreters for the State's diplomatic services in the Levant (these had previously depended on locally hired and often unreliable Greeks), but gradually expanded into a sort of preparatory school for the whole diplomatic service, even the famous *Theresianum*, founded by Maria Theresa herself for the secondary education of the sons of nobles, an institution which maintained itself up to 1918 as the best of its kind in the Monarchy—all were *ad hoc* creations to meet needs which had made themselves felt. So far as existing institutions were concerned, the reforms were almost confined to the Universities: the few enactments of the time relating to lower levels were simply common-sense rulings, as that teachers in elementary schools should be men qualified to teach. In the Universities there had been some cleansing of stables in Prague and Innsbruck during the war, but this again had been simply *ad hoc* correction of specific abuses reported. The systematic and large-scale reforms were triggered off by reports from the Austrian Court Chancellery, in 1748 and January 1749, on conditions in the medical faculty of Vienna University, which showed that owing to the inadequacy of the teaching, and other defects, most students were going abroad to finish their studies. Maria Theresa promptly ordered that no Austrian medical student might take his degree at a foreign University, and appointed a Commission to submit proposals for the reform of the Faculty. One member of this body was Gerhart van Swieten, the remarkable Dutchman whom she had imported in 1745 to be her personal physician; it was he who afterwards became her adviser in chief on educational questions and the *spiritus rector* of all her early reforms in that field.

Van Swieten sent in his proposals within a few days, and Maria Theresa adopted them on the spot, unaltered, and appointed him head of the Faculty, to carry them through. Next, with him advising her, she had the Faculties of Theology and Philosophy reorganised on similar principles in 1752, and that of Law in 1753; subsequently, the reforms were extended to Innsbruck, Prague, Graz and Freiburg.

The changes were very extensive. Old abuses and short-comings in the administrative systems were swept away, so that students could receive regular instruction and graduate without undue delay or expense. Teaching methods were reformed, and curricula enlarged by the establishment of new chairs in such subjects as history, geography, civics and the natural sciences. 1752 even saw the foundation of a chair of German Rhetoric, the first holder of which, incidentally, was a Slovene. The Law Faculty received a chair of Natural Law. Even in philosophy there was a perceptible shift, due in particular to the influence of Christian Wolff, towards a more modern and realistic approach. The whole system was placed firmly under State control. Early on in the process, the rule was established that appointments to chairs were made by the Crown. Later, the State took over the whole administration of the Universities' finances.

These reforms, like their counterparts in the political field, were carried through with a handsome disregard of ancient autonomous rights and vested interests, and like them, brought many salutary results. Standards of instruction improved enormously, and the instruction itself became more purposeful. Not the smallest of the gains were those made by the teaching profession itself, for the order introduced into the Universities' finances, which had been in a lamentable condition (most of them had accumulated heavy debts, which were cancelled), made it possible to raise the Professors' stipends substantially, besides which the University of Vienna received handsome new premises, Maria Theresa's own gift.

These changes brought with them not only the transference of the control over the educational system from the hands of the Church to those of the State, but also a considerable amount of laicisation, for not only were the curricula broadened, but a number of the new chairs were, of necessity, given to laymen. Naturally, they struck a heavy blow at the authority of the Orders, particularly of the Jesuits, of whom van Swieten was a declared and embittered enemy. It should, however, be emphasised that their purpose was purely practical. The new bureaucratic State which was coming into being required of its servants a different mental equipment from that which the Jesuits were able to inculcate. It would be entirely mistaken to read into the changes any hostility on the part either of Maria Theresa herself, or of van Swieten, who was a most devout Catholic, to the Catholic religion as such. If Maria Theresa needed useful citizens, it was and remained her life-long conviction that a man could not be a good citizen, at least of her State, if he was not also a good Catholic. The new text-books were closely scrutinised to ensure that they contained nothing contrary to religion, and the rule was long maintained that non-Catholics could not graduate at Universities in the Monarchy, with the result that until the travel ban was lifted for them, Hungarian Protestants could not graduate at all. The control over minds was now actually tightened even outside the educational sphere, for in 1753 Maria Theresa established State censorship over all works, profane as well as religious, published in or imported into her dominions. The control was strict, and can freely be called narrow-minded, for, more like her grandson in this respect, as in many, than is usually admitted, Maria Theresa had no use for abstract learning, nor for the humanities as such: she rejected a proposal for the foundation of an Academy of Sciences, on the ground that it would probably be a breeding-ground for heresies.

There was no more hostility to religion in Maria Theresa's firm assumption, immortalised in her famous dictum to the Archbishop of Vienna: 'Education is and remains a *politicum*', i.e. an administrative question, of State control over the educational system. It was simply the natural parallel to the similar control being established, at the expense of the Estates, over the political system. In this, as in other respects, she took a robustly

Erastian view of Church-State relations. Most pious in her own conduct and assiduous in her devotions, she demanded the same standards of her family, her Court, and indeed, all her subjects. She was puritanical in her condemnation of licentiousness, and insisted that everywhere the Church should be respected and its rules followed. She thought it her duty to uphold and enforce Catholicism in her dominions, as a condition not only pleasing to God but also salutory to man, and she was ruthless to the point of bigotry, and beyond it, in enforcing this rule, except in the few places in which exceptions were allowed by prescriptive right.

But if she regarded Church and State as partners, she drew as clear a line as that traced by any of her House, even her son (only he drew it in a different place), between their respective functions, and was quite unhesitant in asserting her supremacy in what, perhaps out of family tradition, possibly even as the result of early teaching,[1] she regarded as her own field. She imposed taxation on the Church's lands, limited the jurisdiction of the ecclesiastical Courts and withdrew from the churches which possessed it the right of asylum, forbade visitations of Houses in her dominions by the Superiors of Orders whose headquarters lay outside them, and unhesitatingly exercised the *Placetum Regium* to forbid the publication in her territories of Papal Bulls or Brieves of which she disapproved. Far too clear sighted not to be aware of the gap which often prevailed between the theory of religion and the practice of its exponents, she warned her children against making further donations to the clergy, 'because, on the one hand, they do not need it, and on the other, those in possession of donations unfortunately do not employ them as they should, and therewith oppress the

[1] Oddly enough, the books out of which the Jesuits taught her history had taken the Emperor's side in their account of the Investiture Struggle.

public sorely. For no House keeps within the limits of its foundation charter, and many idlers are received.' Later in her reign, she fixed a lower age limit of 24 for entry into a monastery or nunnery.

Another point on which she enforced an alteration of Church rules—this time, indeed, only after obtaining the consent of the Holy See, which she wrung from it, after prolonged and difficult negotiation—was that of public holidays. The argument used to convince the Pope was actually that the interest of Catholicism, threatened as it was by the Protestant power of Prussia, could not be defended without a larger army, and that the people could not support this unless it worked harder. The consent came finally in 1745, when 24 holidays were abolished: attendance at Divine Service was compulsory on those days, but after that, any kind of work was permissible, although landlords were not allowed to exact compulsory service on them.

In yet another field, the separation of the administration from the judiciary brought to light the exceedingly defective condition of the law, both civil and criminal, in the Monarchy, and still more, of the administration of justice; also the wide variations in both respects prevailing between one Province and another. In 1752 two Commissions were set up, one for civil law, the other for criminal law and procedure, their duties being to compare the different systems, select the best in each, and produce comprehensive and uniform codes. Neither of them had by the end of the period completed its work to Maria Theresa's satisfaction, but in the meantime considerable improvements had been introduced into the administration of justice, especially on its lowest level, of the Manorial Courts, and facilities for appeal from questionable decisions had been greatly increased.

Of the finances of the period it is impossible, in default of published figures, to say more than that they improved. Haugwitz' reforms brought about a substantial increase in the yield of the Provincial contributions; furthermore, war-time taxes, including a graduated poll tax imposed in 1746, were maintained into the peace years, and even new ones imposed; another innovation, a State lottery, produced substantial further sums. According to the Venetian Ambassador's estimate, the Crown revenues rose from only 20 million gulden in 1745 to 40 nine years later. Unfortunately, expenditure rose with it. Under her husband's sharp eye, Maria Theresa conscientiously cut down her own spending. Possessed as she was of a full share of the family, and contemporary, passion for building, she could not resist going on with the extension of Schönbrunn Palace, but the work was, after all, spread over 20 years and the cost of it borrowed, through the mediation of Silva Tarouca, from a Portuguese Jewish banker (it was not taken out of the English subsidies, as had been alleged). But she spent little on clothes or jewellery for herself, and the general 'Court Expenditure' was cut from 3,703,000 gulden in Charles' day to 2,780,000 in 1747. This appellation, moreover, covered such items as the cost of foreign missions; expenditure on music for the Court was reduced from 145,000 gulden to 77,000; for food and drink, from 361,000 to 288,000; for general purchases for the Court, from 244,000 to 100,000.

But she was far too truly her father's daughter not to be open-handed, particularly where she—or they—thought individual servants of hers worthy of reward. She put up Uhlfeld's salary for him, on his own application, from 24,000 to 40,000 gulden and paid his debts to the tune of 97,000 more; gave Bartenstein and Silva Tarouca 100,000 each on their retirements, Daun 250,000, Chotek 300,000 for a house, and later, very large sums to Kaunitz, besides innumerable smaller benefactions. Thus between one thing and another, the two ends never quite met. The deficits became smaller, but there was no year quite without one.

These few main headings cannot cover all the internal reforms to which Maria Theresa put her hand during these busy years, for success had mounted to her head, and she had become more than a little nosey, and much more than a little bossy and autocratic. Economy, efficiency, productivity and austerity were the watchwords of the day, and she enforced them with an entirely high hand, brushing opposition aside and blandly ignoring ancient prescriptive rights with the argument that her oath bound her to observe only such rights as were 'ancient and honourable' and left her free where those adjectives were inappropriate. Her subjects got something of a feeling of being watched by Big Sister. It seems probable that the 'Chastity Commission' which gave rise to so much tongue-wagging was really, at least in its main functions, what later German officialdom called *Sittenpolizei*, an organisation for the control of prostitutes. But it is true enough that lapses from austerity by persons of either sex, however highly placed, were visited with Royal displeasure or actual punishment. It is said that Königsegg, as President of the War Council, was ordered to prohibit officers from visiting houses of ill-fame under pain of denial of advancement. The old Field-Marshal replied that if that rule had been in force in his youth, he would still be an ensign. In general, fêtes and gaieties, not those of the Court alone, were cut down, both in Vienna and in the country-side, where many innocent forms of merrymaking were prohibited, either as time-wasting and leading to 'excessive gaiety and sinful living', or as superstitious, and the latter excuse was invoked to ban many more traditional usages which might, perhaps, be called superstitious but were nevertheless treasured parts of rural life.

Very much of all this was, of course, highly unpopular. It went without saying that the great aristocrats resented bitterly seeing their political powers clipped and their income reduced for the benefit of the new bureaucracy, just as the ex-holders of sinecures and other beneficiaries of Charles' careless housekeeping mourned their lost pickings. But the discontent was not limited to high, and often undeserving, circles. It extended to the subordinate officials, disciplined and set to ever new tasks; to the old-style teachers and to that considerable fraction of the monks and parochial clergy who, untouched by the Jansenism which coloured the more advanced ecclesiastical thought of the day, regarded many of the new measures as positively anti-Christian; to the Viennese shop-keepers and artisans, whose livelihoods had depended largely on the spendings of the Court; even to the peasants, harried by Circle officials to be more productive. The reduction of the holidays produced a real revolt in Vienna, where men whom Maria Theresa had ordered to work on the second of the three traditional Easter holidays were mobbed and shops which had opened had their windows smashed. That particular order had to be repealed: in any case, it had been generally ignored in the countryside.

The whole population, naturally, grumbled when taxation, instead of going down with the coming of peace, was actually raised.

The chief objects of the popular wrath were Haugwitz, the man from nowhere, the upstart and newcomer to Austria and Catholicism, and his band of 'Silesian quill-drivers'. It was particularly unfortunate that Haugwitz was, as it happened, a man of conspicuously unpleasing exterior and manners. A mob pelted his house with stones and excrement, and he had to be assigned an armed guard to protect him. But the resentment, of high and low, did not spare Maria Theresa herself; one may, indeed, wonder what her reputation in history would have been had she died now (and would Joseph have mellowed had Fate granted him a life as long as hers?). She herself became aware of the decline in her popularity, and asked Silva Tarouca the reasons for it, and he did not deny the fact, although the reasons he gave were (except that he blamed her for indulging her passion for cards while restricting the pleasures of others) mainly of a nature to do her credit: that she was working too hard, showing herself too little, in fact, taking life too seriously. She went ahead.

IV

All this internal consolidation had, as has been emphasised, been carried through, primarily, as a means to an end: the recovery of Silesia, and the complement to it would have to be the existence of the appropriate international situation. Could Austria achieve her aim, could she even escape further losses, without changes in this respect? In March, 1749, thus immediately after she had put the coping-stone on her great administrative reorganisation, and only a few months after the conclusion of the Peace of Aix-la-Chapelle, Maria Theresa invited the members of her Privy Conference to submit their views in writing whether Austria's old system of alliances with the Maritime Powers should be maintained, or exchanged for another.

Six members of the Conference, including Francis—the others were Harrach, Uhlfeld, Khevenhüller, Colloredo and Königsegg—were for maintaining the old system, as the only counter-weight to the predominance of France, and in particular, the only safeguard of Austria's possession of the Netherlands. Francis went so far as to advocate good-neighbourly relations with Prussia. There was only one dissentient: Count Wenzel

Anton von Kaunitz, a rising young diplomat, whom, on his return from Aix-la-Chapelle, where he had been representing Austria's interests, Maria Theresa had, despite his relative youth—he was then in his 47th year— appointed to the Conference. In a very long, reasoned memorandum, Kaunitz argued that Prussia was the worst, most dangerous and most irreconcilable enemy, not only the robber of Silesia, but the menace to Austria's whole position in Europe. The Maritime Powers, although indeed Austria's natural allies, would be unable or unwilling to help her against Prussia, but France could, and should, be induced to do so, even if this involved the sacrifice of minor territories in Italy, or of part of the Netherlands. An alliance with France would also secure Austria the support of the Middle German States, such as Saxony and the Palatinate.

By virtue of this memorandum, and of his subsequent activities, Kaunitz is usually credited with the official paternity of the famous *renversement d'alliances* which followed: but Maria Theresa's own mind had certainly been moving in the same direction. She herself writes, in the passage quoted on an earlier page, that 'after she saw that she must put her hand to the Peace of Dresden' ... 'the system of this House altered completely, in that formerly it had held the balance against France and now this ceased to be a consideration', which was why she wanted the war to end quickly, 'even if it cost her losses in the Netherlands and Italy', and it is obvious that in 1746 she felt much more bitterly against Britain than against France. Her instructions to Kaunitz at Aix actually contain the words that 'whatever one might think of France, the King of Prussia must be regarded as a far more dangerous hereditary enemy to the Arch-House.' It is quite possible that her reason for promoting Kaunitz to the Conference was that she knew that he would advise a policy on which she was already decided; it is not even excluded that the ambitious young diplomat cut his policies to her known wishes. In any case, she opted for him, and after some of the dissentients had been brought round, the new policy was launched, Kaunitz himself being sent to Paris as Ambassador to put out the first feelers.

The negotiations got under way only very slowly. Kaunitz' first reception in Paris was so chilly that in 1751 he actually wrote to Maria Theresa that the task was impossible: better go back to the old line. At home, most of Maria Theresa's other advisers, including Kaunitz' official superior, Uhlfeld, were against him. She, however, would hear of no recantation, and although she recalled him from Paris, it was to make him head of foreign affairs, dismissing in his favour not only Uhlfeld but also Bartenstein, with whom Kaunitz had refused to work. To fortify his prestige, she bestowed on him the title, held after him, in all Austrian history, only by Metternich, of 'Chancellor of State' (*Staatskanzler*).

Active pursuit of the new course was in fact shelved for a couple of years, and overt signs of hostility to Prussia eschewed; indeed, when the Czarina of Russia tried to spur her ally into attacking Frederick, whom she detested, she was tactfully repressed. But Kaunitz never seriously renounced his intention, in spite of the big difficulty—besides that of winning France over—that Britain was Austria's ally, and so far had shown no signs of ratting on the alliance: it had, on the contrary, spent considerable sums on subsidising the Electors to the Imperial Crown, to ensure Joseph's succession on his father's death.

Then, in March, 1755, after clashes between British and French colonists in Canada had made war between the two mother-countries seem imminent, Britain, invoking the 'Barriers Treaty', called on Austria to contribute a substantial force for the defence of the Netherlands. This was the moment when the ways parted, and one of them had to be chosen. A decisive Crown Council on June 12 heard Kaunitz argue that a maritime war would inevitably develop into a land one, in which Austria's first move must be to attack Prussia with all the force she could muster. The reply to Britain, sent only in June, did not refuse the request outright, but set an intolerably high price on it. Meanwhile, Starhemberg, Kaunitz' successor in Paris, was instructed to make such proposals to Louis as to tempt him into an alliance: even territorial concessions in the Netherlands and Italy might be offered. When he reported that Louis was best approached through the Pompadour (with whom Kaunitz had already made friends), Maria Theresa herself authorised the use of that channel. Louis was still wavering, uncertain whether Austria would prove a more profitable partner than Prussia, when Frederick himself, alarmed above all by Britain's agreements with Russia, approached Britain with offers which led to the conclusion on January 16, 1756, of the 'Convention of Westminster', which pledged the two countries 'to unite their forces to prevent the entry or passage' of 'whatsoever foreign Power upon whatsoever pretext desires to march its forces into Germany'—an agreement which amounted to a guarantee by Britain of Silesia and by Prussia of Hanover.

The Convention did, indeed, exclude the Netherlands, but since, even so, it was purely defensive, and Britain, with other Powers, was already guaranteeing Frederick's possession of Silesia under the Treaty of Aix-la-Chapelle, it is difficult to follow Maria Theresa's logic when, afterwards, she invoked it to argue that Britain, not she, had been false to the British-Austrian alliance. But it proved the immediate solvent of that instrument. For now it was France's turn to feel anxious, and on May 1, 1756, she signed with Austria the 'First Treaty of Versailles', which pledged Austria to neutrality in a war between France and Britain, and France, to the same attitude in case of an attack on Austria by Prussia or the Porte, while under a second, secret, article, France agreed to provide 24,000 men to help Austria in that event. Negotiations now opened on France's price for more active intervention: she asked for the whole of the Austrian Netherlands, which Kaunitz was willing to concede only if the war left Austria in undisputed possession of Silesia and Glatz, and if France helped her actively to achieve this. Meanwhile the Czarina had, in March, already proposed an offensive alliance, promising, if Austria would attack Prussia, to send 80,000 men and not to rest until Silesia was recovered; she had even begun to arm. Kaunitz had, it is true, advised holding up the Russian treaty until that with France was concluded, and had sent back word to Petersburg that the attack could not begin until the next spring. Meanwhile, however, the negotiations with France were pressed forward, and in May and June certain preparatory measures of military pre-mobilisation were ordered.

Well-informed of all this, through leakages in Petersburg, Frederick sent an emissary to Vienna, saying that he had sure information that Austria had concluded an offensive treaty against him with Russia, and demanding a categorical assurance that she did not intend to attack him, that year or the next. Maria Theresa replied with technical accuracy, although the tone of moral indignation which she used was perhaps less justifiable, that no such treaty existed. Frederick did not believe her, and after sending a last message that he was prepared for an understanding if Austria would make suitable proposals, and receiving no reply, he invaded Saxony on August 29.

PART THREE

THE SEVEN YEARS WAR
1756–1763

I

So began the second great war of Maria Theresa's reign. Whether the 'guilt' for it was hers, or Frederick's, is a question over which Austrian and Prussian historians have wrangled in countless volumes, and it is a barren enough controversy. Obviously, Frederick sparked off the tinder, and as certainly, if one takes the view, as Maria Theresa did, that 1756 only continued what 1740 had begun, then the original guilt, too, was his. But it is equally certain that he was, in truth, only forestalling his enemies. The documents prove to the hilt that they meant to attack him, and Maria Theresa herself admitted, in later years, that the enterprise was one of the type which never brought their authors any good.[1] Austria's trouble was that not only were her diplomatic preparations still incomplete, but her military preparations even more so. It had only been a few weeks since the first orders in this field had gone out, and they had been that regiments should be brought up to strength, the Estates being asked to supply more recruits, and volunteers sought at home and abroad, remounts bought, fortresses put into condition—all measures which would not show results for months. Meanwhile, Austria had only 55,000 men available for immediate field operations, two thirds of

[1] See below, p. 150.

them, under Browne, in Bohemia, the rest in Moravia.
And while it is true that the Austrian army of 1756 was
far superior to the Austrian army of 1740, the relative
gap between its efficiency and that of the Prussian had
not narrowed in anything like the same measure, for
Frederick, too, had been at work, and with more urgency
than the incurably leisurely Austrians.

How completely Frederick took the Austrians un-
aware is shown by the fact that when he moved, Maria
Theresa was away hunting in Hungary; she had, it was
whispered, overcome her distaste for the sport in order to
keep an eye on her husband.

So Frederick reaped the full advantage of his surprise
tactics. He invested the Saxon army at Pirna, near
Dresden, beat off an attempt by Browne to relieve it,
forced it to capitulate and incorporated it into his own
forces. But it was too late for him to invade Bohemia
seriously that year—he entered it, but soon withdrew—
and the next, things went much better for Austria. On
May 1 France signed the Second Treaty of Versailles,
this time an offensive alliance, under which, in return for
the cession, in case of victory, of the Netherlands, partly
to herself, partly to Don Philip of Spain (although Austria
was to get back Parma and Piacenza), she was to put
another 105,000 men, besides the 24,000 first promised, in
the field against Frederick, who on his defeat was to lose
Silesia and Glatz to Austria and other territory to
Saxony and Sweden (which also entered the war).

France's troops moved, as did 80,000 from Russia,
which signed her offensive alliance on May 19. Finally,
an Imperial Diet agreed to contribute an 'army of
execution' against Frederick, as breaker of the *Reichs-
frieden* (peace between members of the Empire). Trying
to snatch a quick victory over the Austrians before the
forces of her allies arrived, Frederick beat the Austrian
army in front of Prague, but failed to take the city, and

was himself defeated by Daun at Kolin on June 18—the first important victory ever won over him by Austrian troops[1] and forced to evacuate Bohemia. Faced now with the armies of Austria, Russia, Sweden, France, and a contingent from the Empire, Frederick's position looked desperate, and would probably have been so had Maria Theresa not conferred the supreme command of her armies on her extremely incompetent brother-in-law, and long retained him in that position when his own brother advised his recall. When, after a year, the popular indignation at last absolutely compelled her to remove him, she insisted on setting her favourite, Daun, in his place; and Daun, good as an organiser and a strategist, unexceptionable as a man, was not indeed as sluggish, but almost as hesitant in the field as Prince Charles. Austria's one dashing general, Laudon, was so junior, and his seniors so jealous of him, that he seldom got a free hand. Thus things degenerated, after all, into a ding-dong struggle. The Austrian soldiers fought much better in this war than the last, and they and their allies won quite a number of victories, one of them, at Kunersdorf, in 1759, so sensational that in Vienna they thought the war over. Saxony and Silesia were cleared, re-lost, cleared again; Berlin itself twice entered. But the successes were hardly ever followed up. Again and again Frederick extricated himself from what seemed hopeless positions, and struck back. 1757, 1758, 1759, 1760 passed, and neither side had beaten the other to its knees.

In October, 1761, Frederick's position was severely weakened when Pitt was succeeded in London by Bute, who was perfectly willing to sacrifice Prussia if by so doing he could more easily conclude a satisfactory peace with France, and in fact, stopped the subsidies. But this

[1] It was in honour of this victory that Maria Theresa founded the military 'Order of Maria Theresa', bestowing on Daun its first Grand Cross.

was more than compensated by the loosening of the ring of Frederick's enemies. France was as ready to jettison Austria as Britain, Prussia; and now that defeat for her overseas seemed inevitable, the Austrian alliance, having failed to prevent this, lost its value for her: on the contrary, a Germany balanced between Austria and Prussia was safer than one dominated by the former. Her troops fought with less than half a heart, and Choiseul adjured Austria to make peace. More important still, Frederick's implacable enemy, Elizabeth of Russia, died in January 1762. The new Czar, Peter, was, on the contrary, a fervent admirer of Frederick's, and not only made peace with him, but actually sent troops to help him. Peter, it was true, was murdered after reigning only six months, and his widow, Catherine, who succeeded him, denounced the alliance and recalled the troops, but she too insisted on peace, which Sweden had already made. Spain, the latest addition to the French camp, soon collapsed.

Austria could not carry on the fight alone, for if Prussia was near-exhausted, so was she. Her tax-payers had been squeezed to the limit of what then seemed possible, the sources of credit had dried up. In July 1762 she had made history by resorting to the issue of paper money,[1] and soon after this, the army was actually reduced, although more on paper than in reality: units were telescoped and the superfluous officers placed on half-pay. In October her troops were driven completely out of Silesia and another force heavily defeated outside Freiburg.

Right up to this point, Maria Theresa had been the

[1] This was necessary because (unlike Frederick) Maria Theresa refused to debase her silver currency. The notes, of which only 12 million gulden were issued, were in fact readily taken at their face value and quietly called in after a few years. It was reserved for the Napoleonic Wars to make the Austrian *Bankozettel* a public hissing.

heart and soul of the war party, both in her own dominions, and in the whole coalition against Prussia. When, in 1758, Frederick came dangerously near Vienna, she had refused to leave the city, forbade the Court to do so, and declared that she would defend the last village, and in the last resort, challenge Frederick to single combat. If, in 1759 she had expressed herself to the French Ambassador as war-weary, this was probably in order to frighten the French into greater activity.

Even now, her utterances show no traces of repugnance against war as such, nor of reluctance to impose on her subjects any sacrifices which she thought it necessary to extract from them. But she was too sensible to go on fighting for a cause which she saw to be lost, and impetuous as she was, when she made turns, they were right-about ones. When she found France negotiating hopefully with Britain, she drew the conclusions, and urged Kaunitz to make peace as quickly as possible: delay would only make things worse, and a bad peace was better than war. On February 8, 1763, 5 days after Britain and France had signed peace in Paris, Austria and Prussia concluded, through the mediation of Saxony, the Peace of Hubertsburg. This restored the territorial *status quo ante bellum*, so that Austria had even to evacuate Glatz, the one area lost at Dresden which her troops had still held. Her only consolation was that Frederick promised to vote for the election of the Crown Prince Joseph to be Roman King, i.e., heir apparent to the Imperial Crown.

* * *

So ended Maria Theresa's second big war; and it makes much less pleasant viewing in retrospect than the first. This time, it is true, she had lost no territory, but even in material respects, in blood and treasure, the cost of the war had been heavy, and all the *imponderabilia* had

gone to her enemy. It was he, this time, who had dazzled
Europe by defying overwhelming odds, snatching victory,
again and again, out of the very jaws of disaster. Her, the
world no longer saw as a romantic and pathetic young
girl, but as a hard, middle-aged woman, in whom it was
not impossible to recognise one of the triad of gossiping
hags—the Pompadour and the libertine Czarina the
other two—who, in Frederick's cruel caricature, were
scheming to divide his lands between them.

Undoubtedly, the war had sent Frederick's stock up
among the German Princes; by the end of it, feeling
among them had changed dramatically in his favour,
and against Austria. Not that he was any better a
'German' than Maria Theresa, if as good; it is a distor-
tion of history to represent him as defending Germandom
against the foreigner, and it was not for their Germandom
that the Princes feared, but for their thrones and their
pockets. But they felt that Maria Theresa had used them
for her own dynastic purposes, and especially the Protestant ones among them were nervous of Austrian
power. Prussia was enough Austria's inferior in strength
to appear to them as their natural protector, while not so
weak, since the acquisition of Silesia, as to be unable to
fill the part, which it did in fact thereafter, for many
decades, until it became strong enough to exchange it for
that of Moloch.

II

Maria Theresa had thrown herself into the conduct of
her second war as whole-heartedly as into that of its
predecessor. Deeply as she was coming to rely on Kaunitz
in foreign policy, she never abandoned her independence
of judgment, even in his favour. All important decisions
were submitted to her, and if she approved them, it was
often with comments, reservations and amendments. In
military matters, not only did she (often in consultation

with Kaunitz) decide the direction of the campaigning for which the international situation called, but also repeatedly sent imperious instructions to her generals on their immediate moves. When they were defeated, she enquired narrowly into the reasons—even Daun had to submit to such an inquisition. She even gave her opinion on technical questions, paying, amongst other things, keen attention to the clothing and supply of the troops, and it may be remarked that on all these points her judgment was often much sounder than that of her military experts. The pity was that she so often nullified them by her over-tenderness towards old friends or intimates, especially in respect of the choice of commanders.

These preoccupations forced her to lay aside her domestic planning programmes, and the internal history of the war years consisted chiefly of hand-to-mouth expedients for raising money. They did, however, see a few re-adjustments and innovations on the top level. When her financial difficulties became acute in 1759 and almost intolerable in 1760, she appealed to Kaunitz, in whose sagacity she had come to place an almost unlimited confidence, to find her a solution. Kaunitz might have answered that Austria's remedy was to break off a war which she could not afford, and ought never to have provoked. But this would have meant admitting that he had himself been at fault, and he preferred to attack the system which had been established by Haugwitz, of whom he was deeply jealous. It was a fact that the great Directorate had become over-dimensioned: it had taken in one department after another until it had become responsible for almost all public business, except foreign affairs and military operations, and it did not possess the expert staff to deal with many of them. Either questions were neglected, or they got assigned to *ad hoc* 'Commissions', which reported independently to the Crown.

The result was a renewed tangle of competences, in which the financial departments, in particular, were finding their business held up. The War Commissariat, above all, had undoubtedly lost in efficiency since being taken over by the Directorate. On the other hand, Hungary, the Netherlands and the Italian Provinces lay altogether outside the competence of the Directorate.

Kaunitz rightly pointed out that there existed no institution in the Monarchy in a position to survey its problems as a whole, and that the whole field was too vast for a single person to master. He proposed the institution of an advisory Council of State (*Staatsrath*), to be composed of the Chancellor (presiding), three members of the higher nobility and three of the lower. None of the civilian members, except the Chancellor himself, was to have any departmental responsibilities, so that their advice should not be slanted by the interest of their own departments. They were to give impartial advice on all subjects submitted to them. Their competence was to extend to the entire Monarchy.

Maria Theresa adopted the idea with enthusiasm, and the members of the Council were appointed, first among them being Haugwitz. He could not have been passed over, but at the same time, the non-departmental condition meant, as Kaunitz had obviously intended, that he had to resign from the Presidency of the Directorate, so that the way was clear for a redistribution of functions. Foreign Affairs and the War Council retained, of course, their independence, as did the Supreme Court of Justice, but the Directorate was abolished. In its place a new 'Court Chancellery' was set up for administrative questions, while finance reverted to the control of no less than three different bodies: the re-emergent Camera, which resumed independent charge of the collection and administration of the revenues from the Crown properties and monopolies; a 'Credit Deputation', for a time known as the *Caisse Générale*, into which receipts were paid, and which was in charge of all debt and credit operations; and the *Hofrechnungskammer*, or Court of Audit. The *Kommerzienrat*, or Economic Council, again became an independent Ministry, and again, competent for the whole Monarchy.

A little later (in 1763) the Provincial 'Deputations' were replaced by *Gubernia* (Governments), each under a President appointed by and responsible to the Crown, and each containing sections for the local administrative, judicial and financial services. The Circle Offices were left untouched.

The importance of most of these changes was, indeed, more apparent than real. The financial and economic portfolios underwent, as will be seen, a fresh re-allocation only three years later. The administrative and financial services were re-united by Joseph II in 1782, only to be separated again by Leopold I in 1791, and thereafter the two met and parted again like a pair of Hollywood actors. For the rest, the importance of the operation lay, not in what it changed, but in what it left untouched. When the State Council debated whether agenda should be divided locally, or by subjects, Maria Theresa declared herself 'unalterably opposed' to any reversion to the former system, so that the new administrative Ministry, the official title of which was 'the United Bohemian-Austrian Court Chancellery', remained competent for both groups of Provinces, as did the Court of Justice. The principle of dualism remained unaltered also in its outward-looking aspect, for neither body was competent outside this area, and Hungary even objected successfully to being placed under the control of the Council of State. The device had to be adopted of calling in a Hungarian 'assessor' when affairs of the Kingdom were under discussion.

Most important of all, the essentially bureaucratic composition of the system underwent no diminution.

When the new Government was set up in Bohemia, the local nobles had high hopes that Kaunitz would put it back in their hands; but he himself wrote to the Empress:

'I cannot advocate putting the nobles and the Estates back in their high places. I am myself a Bohemian noble and landed proprietor, but my duty to Your Majesty comes first. How dangerous the powers of the nobles are, has shown itself in Hungary, Transylvania and the Netherlands. I must confess before God and Your Majesty that I regard the reintroduction of rule through the nobility as something which would, at a blow, cut off all improvements and hopes, and deal a most sensible blow to Your supreme power.'

In fact, the following years saw a further diminution of the powers of the Estates: the new war taxes and taxes on capital then introduced were decided and levied without consultation or co-operation with the Estates.

For the State Council: there was obviously room in a country which possessed no Parliament and not even a political Press, for some institution composed of people with no axe to grind in which the proposals of bureaucratic heads of departments could be scrutinised and weighed against each other, and the Council undoubtedly did good work on its first great problem, and on some later occasions. The danger was always that it might become over-burdened with detail and degenerate into a mere blend of fifth wheel, bottle-neck and sugar in the petrol, whereby heads of departments who knew their business found proposals made by them held up indefinitely for comment by amateurs. Joseph, who was immediately admitted to membership of it, held that view of it (as will be seen) from the first; later, the question whether it was an asset or a nuisance occupied much of the time of Francis I and his advisers.

Another obvious weakness in Kaunitz' work was that it left the Monarchy without a Ministerial Council, such as the Privy Conference (which had faded inconspicuously out of existence) had, after its fashion, constituted. This gap, not apparently noticed by Maria Theresa in 1761, soon made itself felt, but the various devices adopted to fill it belong, again, to a later chapter of Austrian history.

*   *   *

The little time which Maria Theresa could spare from public business was now spent chiefly with her huge family, of which the 15th member, the ill-fated Marie Antoinette, was born in November 1755, thus on the eve of the war, and the 16th and, as it proved, last, Maximilian Franz, in December 1756, thus when the war was already in full swing. Besides the three who had died before the war broke out, she lost two more—Karl Joseph and Joanna—in the course of it, but 4 boys and 7 girls were alive at the end of it. It was no self-flattery when Maria Theresa described her heart, as she often did, as maternal, and she was a devoted and assiduous mother to all this enormous brood, and seldom failed to spend part of her day with them.

As the elder among them began to grow up, she also had to think about their educations. This was, indeed, entrusted to specialists, but she scrutinised their progress reports with great care, and even took the pains to plough through the primer on Austrian history which Bartenstein had, on her orders, compiled for the use of Joseph. It was the education, intellectual and moral, of Joseph which was, of course, the most important task, and it did not prove easy. Some of his tutors accused him of lack of application and even of slowness in the uptake, which seems extraordinary, for he was certainly not stupid, nor, in his later years, idle, whatever else he was. The truth probably was that he revolted against the unmerciful cramming to which he was subjected. But he also early gave indications of the ugly faults which marred his character as a man: self-will, conceit, obstinacy and 'a tendency to pick out and make fun of people's physical short-comings or inner defects.' Maria Theresa was far too shrewd to be blind to his faults, and although she loved him tenderly, she repeatedly warned his tutors not to be soft with him. Once she even ordered him to be whipped, replying, when his shocked tutor protested that such an indignity had never been inflicted on an Arch-duke: 'Yes, and look how they turned out!' Joseph seems nevertheless to have returned her affection: there are no traces in his childhood years of the conflicts which were so common between the grown man and his mother. But he was unmistakably an unpleasant boy, who grew on into an unpleasant young man, and even very early displayed views horrifying to his mother on various subjects: an unpious rationalism, and worst of all, an admiration for the arch-enemy, Frederick of Prussia.

Joseph might still have turned out relatively human but for a deep personal tragedy which befell him in earliest manhood. The line had to be continued: he had to marry, and his marriage was arranged over his head as completely as those of his brothers and sisters after him. The bride picked for him was Isabella, Duchess of Parma, daughter of Philip V of Spain and grand-daughter, through her mother, of Louis XV of France. Although recognising that his marriage must be dictated by *raison d'état*, Joseph had received the news of the agreement without enthusiasm. 'I will,' he wrote to a friend, 'do everything to win her respect and confidence. But love? No!' But as it happened, things turned out differently from expectation. When, in September, 1760, the bride was fetched from her home, she delighted Maria Theresa, and Joseph himself fell passionately in love with her. It was the one human emotion of his life, and a desperately tragic one. Not only does it seem clear today —although it is doubtful whether Joseph knew it—that the only person whom the dark, inscrutable beauty loved —in whatever sense she did so—was Joseph's sister, Maria Christina, but such happiness as she gave her husband was short-lived. After presenting him with a daughter, she died of the small-pox in November, 1763, leaving him desolate.

The blow proved irremediable. Joseph was told that he must marry again, and at first said that the only woman of whom he could bear the thought was his lost Isabella's younger sister, Louise. But even if the problem of the prohibited degree could have been got over, Louise was only a child of 14, and in any case, already betrothed to the Infante of Spain. In the end Joseph accepted and, in January 1765 married the Bavarian Princess, Josepha. It was a wretched decision for them both. The poor little Princess, although amiable enough, was physically unprepossessing. Joseph treated her abominably, and it was a true release for her when she, too, died of the small-pox in the fatal year of 1767.

He refused absolutely to take a third wife; fortunately, his brother Leopold was by this time married, and perpetuating the dynasty as rapidly as Maria Theresa herself had done.

* * *

Her many war-time preoccupations had left Maria Theresa little time for gaiety, and she was also coming to lose gusto for it. As early as 1745 observers had detected in her signs of matronliness, and since then her almost uninterrupted series of pregnancies—although she took them astonishingly lightly—had inevitably told, even on her; her corpulence, too, was growing on her. A further curb was shortage of money; she had sold most of her jewels as a contribution to the war effort.

Nevertheless, she had shown no trace of failing spirits or resistance during the war, nor had she grudged money if the occasion called for the spending of it. The cortège which brought Joseph's bride to him from Italy, in mid-war, indeed, in the hour of some of Austria's most dismal defeats, was one of the most splendid processions that Europe had ever seen.

The unsatisfactory ending to the war saddened her, but although it is probably true that she now sincerely renounced hope of recovering Silesia—she had pronounced this 'a chimera' in 1762—it is not possible to agree with those historians who date the real and deep change of heart which she undoubtedly underwent in her middle years, from the Peace of Hubertusburg. She soon recovered her spirits; and indeed, but for the loss of Silesia, the picture before her was by no means all dark. Economically, her dominions had suffered relatively little—far less than Frederick's. Some of the chief industries were flourishing under the stimulus of war. The public debt had, indeed, swollen to the heavy figure of 270 million gulden, 38 million of it owed abroad and most of it bearing the heavy interest of 6 per cent, while most of the papers were changing hands at a substantial discount. But in September 1763, Maria Theresa put her husband in personal charge of the question. He succeeded in carrying through a conversion from 6 per cent to 5 per cent which brought the papers back almost to their nominal course. It could be hoped that the years would bring a further improvement.

Internationally, Frederick was now on his best behaviour, Catherine still on hers, and the French connection, by which, to the end of her life, Maria Theresa set great store, in process of consolidation, one step towards this being the betrothal of Maria Theresa's second—eldest surviving—son, Leopold, to Maria Luisa of Spain. 'Never since I came into the world,' Leopold wrote to a friend in October 1763, when the news of the King of Spain's consent to the marriage arrived, as well as Frederick's assurance that he would vote for Joseph's election as Roman King and would not interfere in Polish affairs (which the unexpected death of King Augustus had suddenly made acute), 'have I seen Their Majesties in such good humour and so gay. . . . The joyful mood casts its rays on us all, and I can say that I have never been so happy as I am now.'

Things continued to go well the next year. The necessary votes for Joseph were collected, and he was duly elected and then crowned King; the coronation, over which Joseph chose to make himself facetious, took place on April 3, 1764 (Goethe has left a vivid description of it in the 5th book of his *Dichtung und Wahrheit*). It cost Austria the considerable sum of 3 million gulden, not counting *douceurs* to Electors, but Maria Theresa, who took great pleasure and pride in the event, although she did not attend it, counted the money well spent.

The new machinery was running smoothly in the West, and politically, the only cloud was another disappointment in Hungary. The financial stringency made it absolutely imperative to get a larger *contributio* from Hungary, and there was an obvious case in equity for raising this out of a tax on the nobles' lands; their exemption was, after all, only (in theory) their reward for their obligation to serve in the 'noble levy', and this romantic but dubiously effective force had not in fact been called out in the Seven Years War. The exemption from taxation of the Church's lands was in any case illogical, for the Church enjoyed it only in virtue of the legal fiction which ranked it as a 'noble', while, of course, performing no military service.

When she convoked the Diet, for June 1764, Maria Theresa had high hopes of putting this programme through. 'I hope,' she wrote to the Electress of Saxony, 'that this Diet will go off to my satisfaction. I am very fond of the Hungarian nation, and I believe that my love is returned.'

She had, indeed, been at considerable pains, ever since 1741, to conciliate the Hungarians. She had given high military and diplomatic posts to a number of their leading men, and bestowed on them an even disproportionate number of honours and decorations. For the lesser nobles, she had founded a 'Royal Hungarian Bodyguard', to which each County sent two youths of noble birth. Now she had prepared a programme of economic expansion, including the development of industry and facilities for exports, which was to be Hungary's reward if the nobles agreed to being taxed.

Unfortunately, protocol required that a Diet open with the Royal 'proposals', stated unconditionally. Secondly, Maria Theresa had, not for the first nor the last time, underestimated the weight of the non-personal factor. *Douceurs* to a few of its members could not appease the Diet's irritation at having been left unconvoked for 13 years, with a lengthening list of grievances unremedied. Finally, by an unhappy chance, just as the Diet met there appeared a pamphlet by the Court Librarian in Vienna, a Slovene at that, which was naturally supposed to have been inspired, which sought to prove that the Crown possessed a historic right to impose taxation on the Church, and also drew attention to the anomalous character of the nobles' exemption.

Consequently, the Diet granted only a small increase, to 3,900,000 fl., in the *contributio*, and that after months of bargaining. It flatly refused to accept taxation on noble land, and when Maria Theresa countered its argument that the peasants could not be asked for a larger increase, by proposing that the peasants' obligations to their lords be limited (so as to leave them more time to produce wealth for the State) it rejected that also, saying that the Bohemian peasants were already worse off than the Hungarian. Maria Theresa, on her side, suppressed her economic reconstruction plan and (following her experts' report) rejected all but a handful of the Diet's *gravamina*. Once again, Crown and nation parted in mutual dissatisfaction.

* * *

It had been arranged that Leopold should meet his bride, already married to him by proxy, in Innsbruck in August 1765. After the wedding the couple were to go down to Tuscany, which Leopold, Joseph having formally renounced the succession to it, was to govern for his father until Francis died, when his son would succeed him as Grand Duke. The bridegroom's parents, with Joseph and the two eldest Archduchesses, accompanied him to Innsbruck. The marriage was duly solemnised, but then Leopold fell ill. His parents stayed on in Innsbruck till he should recover. On the evening of August 18th Francis went to the theatre. Walking back to his room, he suddenly faltered and collapsed into Joseph's arms. He was carried into the nearest bedroom—a servant's—and a doctor, hurriedly fetched, opened a vein. But the treatment, if it was the right one, came too late. A few minutes later, Francis was dead.

PART FOUR

THE LATTER YEARS
1763–1780

I

The blow of Francis' death was, literally, almost mortal to his wife. Summoned to the death-chamber, where he had already expired, she stood there speechless, as though frozen, until forcibly removed to her own room, where she lay all night, shaken by convulsive sobs. She had her long hair, one of her beauties, cut short and never again, all her life, dressed in anything but widow's weeds. She divided all her jewels among her children, never thereafter wearing any except pearls. She had the death-chamber made into a chapel, and a nunnery (into which her daughter Elisabeth entered later) erected near-by. Returned to Vienna, she thought for a while of spending the rest of her days in a 'retreat' in Innsbruck. All gaiety left her heart. Half her thoughts were in the past, with her husband; when she died, there was found in her prayer book a scrap on which she had counted the years, months, weeks, days and hours—385,744—of her married life. The rest were turned ever more to the next world: she found it 'sheer intolerable to live in the bustle of this world'. Every day she spent hours on her knees.

As the first shock passed, she abandoned the thought of abdication (although often returning to it later in moments of depression), and soon came to immerse herself in her duties as Monarch even more deeply than before, partly because now she had few other earthly distractions, partly because her conscience pricked her for having wasted time on idle pleasures instead of devoting herself wholly to the task to which God had called her. 'What account have I to render,' she asked, 'for so long a reign?'

The years which followed her bereavement were consequently almost as full as those which had preceeded it, although a further interruption came in the dreadful year of 1767, when the small-pox ravaged her family, carrying off her daughter Josepha and Joseph's wife, besides attacking her daughter Elisabeth and her son-in-law, Albert. She, too, caught the infection, characteristically, through tending her unhappy little daughter-in-law, and at one stage, her life was despaired of. But her extraordinary physical resistance carried her through, and she returned to her self-imposed duties with undiminished self-dedication.

Her conception of the nature of her task had now really changed in several important respects, although the extent of her spiritual transformation has sometimes been exaggerated. It is, for example, not the case that she had become a pacifist in the modern sense of the term. War was a fact of life to her, as to all her generation. She attached great importance to the upkeep of an efficient army—its improvement was the first object to which any surplus funds went—and she would always have been ready to use it for sufficient cause. But now she counted costs and weighed risks more soberly than before, and above all, saw few causes which would justify its use. She had now definitively written off the possibility of recovering Silesia by force of arms. Her high-flown visions of recovering the *avulsa imperii* in the West had been buried with the conclusion of the French alliance, to which all the rest of her life she attached great value; the idea of annexing Bavaria, with the Treaty of Füssen.

So far as Germany was concerned, she was satisfied that her son should succeed her husband as its titular head. She regarded the integrity of Poland as an interest of Austria's and looked on that of the Porte in the same light, having a sensible fear of the consequences of tampering with that frail structure, besides a sterling lack of interest—one of her most admirable qualities—in aggrandisement for its own sake; mere numbers and acres did not appeal to her.

In international affairs, she therefore genuinely made the preservation of peace the first aim of her policy, and this affected also her internal policies. Her objectives were still consolidation, centralisation and the affirmation of the Monarchic authority, but no longer with the ulterior object of using them for war. This brought about a shifting of priorities, and a change of emphases, as a result of which the reforms of her later years were more broadly conceived, and went deeper, than their predecessors. Here again there was no question of a sudden and radical change of outlook. Maria Theresa did not suddenly become a liberal or a democrat. All her life she never questioned the rightness of the hierarchical class structure in which she had been brought up, nor did she ever move from her essentially unsentimental and utilitarian point of view: *raison d'état* and practical considerations continued to govern all her policy. But as her outlook grew wider with the years and her experience deeper, she became aware of problems, notably those relating to the peasant population, the very existence of which had escaped her in her youth and since she brought to the solution of these, too, the strong sense of justice which never failed her, her reforms of these years do contain a social element lacking in the earlier series.

Behind this lay a real change of outlook of which she may herself not have been fully aware. Say what one may, her two great wars had been dynastic ones. She had simply, and unhesitatingly, mobilised her peoples for the defence of her throne: when she writes in her *Testament* that one reason why she fought on in the first was her conviction 'that no worse fate could befall her Provinces than to fall into Prussian hands', this must, one fears, be written off as self-deception. But she was now genuinely coming to feel a sense, not only of her cause being that of her peoples, but of theirs as being hers. The *General Instructions* for the reorganised United Chancellery (written, indeed, as early as 1763) lay down that 'Our own welfare is inseparably bound up with that of Our subjects, wherefore the increase of the Monarchic power and revenues cannot be sought except in the furtherance of the common welfare and prosperity.' As written, these words probably only testify to the deeper appreciation of economic realities that was now hers, but they do also reflect a real identification of herself with her subjects such as her father had—to his cost and hers—never achieved. With it, her peoples ceased to be mere instruments of policy; they became objects of it.

For the rest, the reforms relating to the peasants were the only field in which she broke much new ground in these years; in the others, she built further on foundations laid earlier, or even, in some cases, declared further change unnecessary.

*   *   *

An assessment of the record of these latter years of her reign must take into account the other influences operating during it; primarily, that of her son. Joseph was crowned Emperor on his father's death, and therewith the rights and duties connected with the Empire passed to him, formally ceded to him on his coronation by the Empress-Dowager. Immediately after, on September 12, 1765, Maria Theresa made him co-Regent with herself 'over all her Hereditary Kingdoms and Provinces.'

'Co-Regent', as both parties understood the term,

meant simply 'co-adjutor'—the same position as Francis' had been. Joseph was given his special job: in 1766, when Daun, who meanwhile had succeeded to the Presidency of the War Council, died, Maria Theresa put Joseph in special charge of military affairs: not out of any distaste for the job—she told Silva Tarouca that it was 'the one field of administration which interested her'—but because she could not give it the time which its importance deserved. But even here, she by no means abdicated all control: her voluminous correspondence with Daun's successor, Lacy, shows her intervening repeatedly in many questions, especially those of appointments to higher commands. In other fields, she did no more than consult Joseph, if that, or communicate her decisions to him. His signature appeared below hers on official documents, but she required him to append it whether he approved of their contents or not—a demand to which he submitted only after acrimonious argument.

But Joseph was no spiritual re-edition of his father. From the very day of his appointment he plunged into work, receiving Ministers, giving audiences, reading papers, not, indeed, taking decisions, but preparing strongly-worded recommendations for his mother. He burned to put his programmes through, and unfortunately for their relationship, they differed from hers in innumerable respects. He was a man of the 'Enlightenment', all taken up with ideas which seemed to her iconoclastic and even blasphemous: that conscience ought to be free, and that it was the duty of the State to respect its freedom: that noble birth conferred no title to consideration: that historic tradition was negligible, where it was not risible. If she perhaps generalised too little, he went to the opposite extreme: any rule which seemed to him good ought to fit any case, and if it did not, then the case must be altered to fit the rule, and a single instance of a misused institution was the signal for him to attack, not only the individual offender, but the institution as a whole. Moreover, he was autocratic and overbearing, dogmatic, impatient of opposition, intolerably rude to those with whom he disagreed. He was immensely greedy of power, both at home and abroad, and lacking either in his mother's inborn or acquired sense of moderation or in her power to assess realistically the relative strength of the factors involved in any problem.

The co-Regency was consequently a most uneasy business for both parties to it. Joseph was constantly nagging at his mother to adopt his ideas, fretting or flying into tempers and offering to resign when she did not do so. His tone towards her in their correspondence, which is extensive, for he was often away travelling, is always respectful, even servile, but when he opens his heart to others, as to his brother Leopold, his favourite confidant, passionate depths of impatient resentment are revealed. She, in general, keeps her temper with him with a self-command which is rare in her, and must have cost her great efforts, but there are moments when she breaks out, sometimes in lachrymosities, that she, in her turn, would do better to abdicate, failing old woman as she is; at other times—no more classic phrase expresses her attitude so exactly—telling him curtly where he gets off.

How far she in fact modified her policies in deference to his wishes, it is not easy to say. So far as domestic affairs are concerned, very little in the first years; rather more in the last, when her grasp on affairs, and still more, her determination, undoubtedly weakened; but even then, his influence on what was done in this field was only marginal: chiefly, he was studying and preparing for the day when the obstacle would be removed. He was oftener on the winning side in foreign affairs, but this was partly because in some fields of them, where Imperial affairs were concerned, the decisions were constitutionally his to take; in other cases, because his view agreed with that of Kaunitz.

Kaunitz was now not only Maria Theresa's official adviser in chief, in virtue of his offices, on all questions, domestic as well as foreign: he had also acquired over her a personal ascendancy which is not easy to understand, for he was in many respects everything of which she disapproved, or at least, could not appreciate. He was a *Feingeist*, a dabbler in and patron of the arts, steeped in Voltaire and the Encyclopaedists, very far from puritanical in his private life. He was also personally extremely *difficile*, vain and touchy to excess, exceedingly verbose, and on top of this, unpunctual, a late riser and a valetudinarian with a pathological horror of fresh air. He could not bear an open window, and had himself carried to his audiences in a closed sedan. He was also unable to endure the word 'death': if a friend or a colleague died, he had to be told that 'so and so was no longer available'. She was not blind to his absurdities, but she treated him, not only with enormous trust in his devotion and his abilities, but with deep personal affection and forbearance, even going so far as to have the windows shut when he came to see her, a concession which she made to no other human being.

His influence over her was so great that some historians have described the regime as a co-Regency, not *à deux*, but *à trois*, although this phrase both exaggerates the narrowness of its character, and underestimates the extent to which she dominated it. She never hesitated to seek the advice of others besides these two, to over-ride theirs, even in their own fields; just as she corresponded with Lacy over military matters, so she did with Mercy d'Argenteau, her Ambassador in Paris, over Kaunitz' head and behind his back. When, however, they combined against her, she usually, although not always, yielded.

The combination happened most often in foreign affairs: less frequently in domestic, for Joseph, like his father before him, did not like Kaunitz, and Maria Theresa was often called in to smooth down the Chancellor's ruffled plumage. The triangle, such as it was, was an uneasy one.

II

The domestic and foreign problems of this phase, unlike those of its predecessors, were not mutually independent, and the histories of them consequently do not coincide chronologically. If we put the latter last, this is because the first of the two important international crises of the period did not become acute until most of the internal reforms were well advanced, and the ending of it did not affect the nature of the finishing touches put to them after it. The second crisis was nearly the finale of her reign, and was regarded as such by herself.

Before turning either to Maria Theresa's purely domestic policy, or to foreign events in the usual sense of the term, it will be convenient to mention shortly what constituted one of her major preoccupations in the first years of her widowhood: the suitable placing in the world, as they grew up, of her surviving children. Of the 11 still alive in 1765, Joseph and Leopold had already found their niches, and later in the same year the eldest daughter, Marianne, who was clearly unsuited for the marriage market—retiring by nature and physically ailing—took the veil: she died in 1789, Abbess of a convent in Klagenfurt. Maria Christina, the favourite, was married in April, 1766, as soon as the months of deep mourning were over (it was her mother's first public appearance after the tragedy) to Prince Albert of Saxony; Maria Theresa settled Francis' appanage of Teschen on her daughter, and appointed her husband

Vice-Roy of Hungary, where the Palatine had died, with the reversion of the Netherlands (for which the couple had, indeed, to wait for many years). Elisabeth, who had been the beauty of the family, lost her looks in the small-pox epidemic of 1767; then she, too, took the veil, to end her life in Innsbruck, as Abbess of the nunnery founded in her father's memory. It was on the very eve of her marriage to Ferdinand IV of Naples-Sicily that the same disease carried off Josepha. Caroline was promptly substituted for her; the wedding took place the next year. In 1769 Maria Amalia was married off to the young Duke of Parma, five years her junior, while in 1770 the youngest of the daughters, Marie Antoinette, secured the biggest matrimonial prize of all in the person of the heir-apparent to the throne of France. In 1771 Ferdinand was married to Maria Beatrice, the heiress of Modena (formerly destined for Leopold, who had changed fiancées when the death of his brother Charles moved him up in the list); Ferdinand was then sent to govern Lombardy for his mother. Finally, the youngest boy, Maximilian Francis, also entered the Church, to become Prince Bishop of Münster and Elector of Cologne.

Maria Theresa arranged most of these matches with a cold eye to dynastic advantage which shocks a more sentimental age. She made a partial exception only in favour of Maria Christina, her adored 'Mimi', whose eventual husband was her own preferred favourite among several then in the field; but her parents had previously vetoed the man on whom she had first set her choice, Prince Ludwig of Württemberg. Elisabeth, before she lost her looks, was positively hawked round: first she was to have been married to the Polish King, Poniatowski (but the Czarina objected), then to the widowed King of Spain, then actually to the aged and dissipated Louis XV. The unfortunate Caroline suffered bitterly from home-sickness in the first years of her marriage, and of her husband she could say only: 'he is very ugly, but one gets accustomed to that. His character is better than people said.' She described her life as 'a real martyrdom, all the worse because one has to show a contented face to the world. I know now what it is, and I deeply pity Antoinette, for whom it is still to come. I make no concealment that I would rather die than go through again what I have had to endure.' But such was the fate of princesses (and princes) in those days. 'I regard poor Josepha,' Maria Theresa wrote when arranging the match with the horrid little Neapolitan, 'as a victim of policy.' But she went through with the match. In the voluminous correspondence which she kept up to the end of her life with nearly all her children, and which overflows with genuine affection, she never shows a trace of compunction over any domestic misery to which she may have condemned them.

The marriages were political transactions, and meant to serve that purpose, although Maria Theresa seldom tried to pull a definite political wire through her daughters. Once or twice she asked Marie Antoinette to influence her husband in a certain direction, but more often scolded her for meddling in politics. As a rule, her daughters were told to keep their fingers out of affairs of State: their role was to keep up the prestige of their house and their nation by correct, dignified and religious behaviour. She was very lavish with her instructions to this effect: not only her daughters, but her sons and her son-in-law Albert were given elaborate lectures on how to behave, and sometimes she followed these up with later homilies, and on occasion even ordered her Ambassadors to see that they were carried out, or sent special emissaries to do so: she kept up a voluminous correspondence (kept secret even from Joseph and Kaunitz) with Mercy, who then had to advise Marie Antoinette without betraying the source of the counsels.

The tone of these homilies was undoubtedly often dictatorial, even bossy: Leopold, a grown man, father of a family and a ruling sovereign, was told how often he should attend Divine Service, in public and private, how often communicate and confess. It is a tribute to her personality that her orders were nearly always received with appropriate meekness. Marie Antoinette by no means always obeyed them, but only Amalia of Parma revolted openly and insisted on going her own, somewhat flamboyant, way. The result was a rupture of relations between mother and daughter which was never healed.

With the conclusion of the last of these marriages, Maria Theresa could regard her dynastic programme as complete. For some years uncertainty had reigned over the ultimate question of the long-term succession, for after the death of his unhappy second wife, Joseph had steadily refused to marry again, while his own single child, Theresia, died also of the small-pox, in 1770. Fortunately for all concerned, Leopold stepped into the breach. His first child, again, was a daughter, but in February, 1768, a messenger brought to Vienna the glad news that his wife had presented him with a son—tidings which so delighted the Empress that she rushed to the theatre (which she had not previously entered since her husband's death) and electrified the audience by calling out to them, in her broad Viennese: 'Der Leopold hat an Buam (Buben).' Thereafter, Leopold's wife continued to do her duty to the great satisfaction of her mother- and brother-in-law, producing in all 12 sons and 4 daughters, of whom all but two boys and one girl reached maturity.

III

In most fields of home affairs it was for Maria Theresa now really only a question of putting finishing touches, or of defending what she had done before against Joseph's efforts to alter it. There were few more major structural changes, although the financial services were again re-shuffled in 1765. The Camera regained control of the *Caisse Générale*, and for a time, of the Commercial Council, thus re-emerging as a great financial-economic institution, on a par with the Chancellery and Supreme Court. Had Haugwitz lived, he would probably have become almost as influential as ever; as it was, his successor, Count Hatzfeld, who held these posts simultaneously with that of Supreme Chancellor, was one of the most important (and the ablest) figures of these years. But this was, again, only a readjustment of posts within a wider framework which remained unaltered. Hatzfeld's two great portfolios were not reunited. Joseph, who always thought everything done by anyone else wrong, and everyone except himself a fool, opened his co-Regency by sending his mother an enormous memorandum (actually, the second of the series, for he had produced its elder brother four years before) in which he found fault with the entire system as it stood, and nearly all the leading figures in it—he allowed only Kaunitz a certain ability. She simply passed it to the State Council, and nothing whatever happened, except a few personal changes, for several years. In 1773 Joseph, who had been quarrelling with Kaunitz over the administration of Galicia, returned to the charge with a new plan for turning the State Council into 'a real Cabinet for home affairs', and setting up by its side a second 'Cabinet', which should control also the operations of the Court Chancellery. The outcome of a series of shattering rows in which Maria Theresa, Joseph and Kaunitz all in turn threatened abdication or resignation was that the Court Chancellery was left untouched and the State Council had taken off its shoulders a lot of detail-work which it had never been intended to bear.

So the 'system' remained unaltered in its essentials. In

the Western Provinces, the grip of the bureaucracy on the administration was rather tightened than relaxed. More and more duties were assigned to the Governments and Circles, while the functions of the Estates became more and more shadowy. Galicia, after a short transition period, was drawn into the system, placed under the United Chancellery and fitted out with the standard apparatus of *Gubernium* and Circles. The chief variation was that, owing to the reluctance of the Poles to serve under Austria, and Vienna's mistrust, the officials were not, as elsewhere, local men, but men sent up from the German and Bohemian Provinces. For the rest, the régime there during these first years was largely military.

The other areas of the Monarchy remained, as before, outside this system. The Milanese was ruled absolutely enough, and many changes, which cannot be enumerated here, introduced there, but the officials were natives. The Netherlands were allowed to retain their traditional institutions practically intact.

Maria Theresa had been deeply disillusioned by the behaviour of the Hungarian Diet of 1764, and particularly, by the conduct of the magnates, whom she had expected to back her. They had done so over the increased *contributio*, but hardly any of them had supported her over the peasant question, and some of the worst abuses reported to her had been precisely from the estates of the then Palatine, Batthyány, whom she had made one of Joseph's tutors, and loaded with honours. Now she drew the consequences. She did not drop her policy of attracting the magnates by personal favours, but while, on the one hand, she never again tried to draw Hungary into her general system, leaving its taxation system and its institutions unmolested, she also never again convoked a Diet, and put through many reforms which she thought necessary, such as the peasant legislation described below, by the simple method of enacting them by Rescript, *jure majestatis*. When Batthyány died, immediately after the Diet, she left the office of Palatine unfilled, appointing instead another Vice-Roy, in the person of her son-in-law, Albert of Teschen. In her instructions to him she enjoined him, indeed, to show a friendly and conciliatory attitude to all comers, not forgetting the smaller nobles, but the instructions, while completely benignant in tone, contain no hint that the regime over which he was to preside was anything but a benevolent despotism. From this date on she also agreed, with little resistance, to the economic policy described below which revenged itself on Hungary's privileged fiscal position by exploiting the country economically.

* * *

State activity in the field of economics had been given a fresh start by the establishment of the Court Commercial Council in 1762, although that body, again, enjoyed only a short life in the form in which it was established: it was subordinated in the same year to the Camera and absorbed in 1766 into the United Chancellery. Whatever its names, however, it continued very active, although increased experience brought with it a certain diminution of impetuosity in some directions. It was now only in quite exceptional cases that the State tried its own hand as entrepreneur, monopolies were granted less freely, subsidies less incautiously, and there was a certain trend, which was, indeed, reversed again by Joseph a few years later, towards a more liberal trading policy: in 1775 the general level of tariffs was lowered and the list of import prohibitions shortened. There was, however, no change in the general policy of encouraging industry by the grant of licences, subsidies and other facilities, with protection where a case for it could be proved, premiums for new inventions and processes, and inducements to foreign entrepreneurs (some of whom were now rewarded with patents of nobility) and workmen to settle in the country. All the new industries were, as far as possible, built up outside the guilds.

An important step was the abolition in 1775 of all internal tariffs between the German-Austrian and Bohemian Provinces, except the Tirol.

Outside industry and mining, which received much attention, further improvements were made in communications, and much was done in these years to help agriculture by the introduction of better methods of production, improved breeds of sheep and cattle and new plants, such as the potato (which, indeed, the population long and obstinately refused to consume). Maria Theresa took a very lively personal interest in all this. The files of the Camera from 1764 to 1776, which have recently been investigated,[1] show the reports of the Council studded with remarks in her own hand, giving her decisions on points so detailed as the payment to the wife of an English immigrant worker of her travelling expenses to enable her to join him.

They also show that not her son, as is generally believed, but she was the author of the first social legislation in the Monarchy. It is true that most of her enactments in this field are concerned with protecting employers and masters against absconding workers or apprentices. We do, however, find her ordering that children in factories are not to be struck or mishandled, and must receive adequate food: half a pound of meat a day, with soup and sufficient afters, and as much bread as they need 'but not to be taken away or allowed to go bad.'

One way and another, Maria Theresa certainly did more than any Habsburg before, and probably more than any after, her to promote economic progress in her

[1] G. Otruba, op. cit.

Western dominions. The adjective cannot, however, be omitted, for the purposefully anti-Hungarian tendency of the State's economic policy grew stronger than ever with the ascendancy of Kaunitz, who disapproved of Hungary politically and meant to use economic pressure as a political weapon. On his initiative, the State Council resolved in 1761 that 'the equilibrium' (sc. between the financial yields of East and West) 'must be restored by the imposition of other public burdens and the throttling of industry.' In 1763 the Commercial Council advised that no State facilities should be given to any Hungarian enterprises; in 1768 it asked Maria Theresa to prohibit even private individuals from founding factories in Hungary where there seemed any possibility that their products would compete with Austrian. Maria Theresa always refused to sanction any technical discrimination between one of her Provinces and another, but after her disillusionment in 1764 she was ready enough to accept the principle of 'restoration of equilibrium'. 'No alteration,' she wrote then, in reply to a request for facilities for the export of wine, 'to be granted to Hungarian exports and foods: everything to be left as it was before the Diet. . . . No further favours, since the big men, who would be the only ones to profit thereby, have not deserved it!' In practice, the Austrian authorities were able, by the employment of such devices as the over-valuation of Hungarian products at the Austro-Hungarian customs line (which was maintained) to bring the industrial development of Hungary, outside the Cameral properties, to a near-standstill. This was the more oppressive to Hungary because, especially after the Partition of Poland, most of the foreign outlets for its agricultural products themselves had now been blocked. Almost all of these had to go through Austria, and were sacrificed to Austrian interests. If the wheat harvest in Austria was good, wheat coming from Hungary was taxed heavily on the frontier; if the harvest was poor, Hungarian wheat was admitted duty-free into Austria, but the export of it elsewhere prohibited. One order actually forbade Austrian merchants to sell Hungarian wine abroad unless they accompanied it with an equal quantity of Austrian wine. The traditional export of cattle to Italy, driven on the hoof through Styria and Carinthia, was made so difficult that the Venetian merchants took to importing their supplies from Bosnia, via Albania, while Hungary was left, as its people complained, 'choking in its own fat.'

* * *

The reforms enacted by Maria Theresa in favour of the peasants were perhaps the most widely and enduringly beneficial of all carried through by her in this period, or indeed, in all her reign, and they also, as we have said, broke new ground more than any others. Her earlier measures in this field, important as some of them (such as the prohibition of conversion to demesne land) had been, had not constituted any reasoned whole; it is even doubtful whether the new vigilance of the Circle officials had brought the peasants much real benefit, accompanied as each relaxation of the manorial screw had been by another turn of that of the State. At any rate, one of Maria Theresa's most admiring biographers admits that it was generally received with apathy or even hostility.[1]

The reforms of this second period were much more systematic, and while it must be admitted that Maria Theresa's motives in initiating them were, as usual, mainly economic, and in continuing them (to judge from her correspondence), largely fear of revolution, yet it would be unjust to deny the presence in her mind of humanitarian considerations, which certainly strongly influenced some of her advisers.

[1] Arneth IV 39.

The question, to which little attention had been paid since the outbreak of war in 1756, was reopened by the refusal of the Hungarian Diet of 1764 so to restrict their peasants' obligations to their lords as to enable them to produce a higher *contributio* for the State. Maria Theresa decided to find out what the real position was, and when her intention was known, an organised flood of petitions came in to the effect that many landlords, including some of the largest, were imposing on their peasants far heavier burdens than the law allowed. There were also some serious outbreaks of unrest. Maria Theresa had these put down with a heavy hand, but had a survey carried through and the law carefully investigated. Several of her advisers, including Joseph, wanted her to take extreme measures of expropriation which would break the power of the nobles. This she refused to do: 'I do not,' she wrote, 'see either the necessity or the justice of destroying the Hungarians under the curious pretext of preserving the larger part' (sic); but on January 26, 1767, she issued, *jure majestatis*, an *Urbarium* which forbade further conversion from peasant to demesne land, laid down how many acres of arable, grass, etc. constituted a full peasant holding, and codified the exact sum and nature of obligations which a lord could exact from his peasants, graduated according to the size of their holdings (full, half, quarter, cottagers, etc.). She did not alter the existing law, to maintain which she felt herself bound by her oath, but she forbade strictly any infringement of it.

She now began to extend her enquiries to the Western Provinces: as early as 1767 an official in Silesia was sending in proposals on how the conditions of the peasants there could be improved, and in 1768 Maria Theresa ordered similar enquiries to be made in Styria, whence a number of complaints had been coming in. In the next year or two several reforms of detail were enacted in most of the German-Austrian Provinces: the peasants were permitted to trade freely with their produce, some compulsory dues and personal services were abolished, and the penal powers of the Manorial Courts further restricted. Meanwhile, in 1769, severe unrest had broken out in Silesia, and a report on conditions there reached the State Council which drove one Councillor to the characteristic surprised remark, 'that is even worse than in Hungary!' In fact, the Silesian peasants' legal obligations were considerably heavier than the Hungarians'. A Commission of Enquiry was sent up to Silesia, and on the basis of its report a '*Robot* Patent', so called because the principle issue at stake was that of the *robot* or compulsory labour service[1] (the name *urbarium* was confined to cases where a land survey was carried through), was issued for that Province in 1771. Patents on the model of the Silesian were issued for Lower and Upper Austria and Styria in 1772. Then came a delay, owing to the tenacious opposition of the Bohemian landlords, who, however, were forced to yield after two successive famine years had produced dangerous unrest. A Patent for Bohemia was issued in 1775 and extended to Moravia in the same year, and later also, provisionally, to Galicia. Carinthia got its Patent in 1778, Croatia and the Bánát (*urbaria*) in 1780. By Maria Theresa's death all her dominions had been covered except the Littoral, the Tirol, the Netherlands and the Italian Provinces, where Patents were thought unnecessary, Transylvania, where the authorities had not got down to making a survey, although regulations limiting the *robot* were issued in 1768, and Carniola, another laggard, whose turn, however, came in 1782.

All of them were constructed on the same pattern and

[1] From the Slavonic *robota*, meaning work. The exploitation was often heaviest where the *robot* was exacted in the form of industrial labour.

roughly the same principle. When the Silesian Patent was being drafted, one exceptionally progressive member of the Commission, Councillor Blanc, had wanted to have it based 'not on what the law was, but on what it ought to be', and got inserted into the preamble a statement 'that the peasant's conditions must be kept on such a level as to enable him to support himself and his family, and also to produce the revenues needed by the Crown in time of peace or war.' Maria Theresa quite accepted this principle, and laid down the rule that no law must be perpetuated which was unduly burdensome to the 'subject'. In fact, the Silesian Patent contained some modifications of the existing law. Most of the Estates, however, resisted bitterly any modification of their existing rights, and according to the Commissions of Enquiry, it was not the law of which the peasants themselves usually complained, but of the abuses of it and of burdens imposed on them which the law did not sanction. As a general rule, therefore, the Austrian Patents, like the Hungarian, left unmodified the central provision of the number of days' *robot* which could be exacted—usually 156 in a year of haulage *robot*, for the occupant of a full peasant holding; proportionately less for occupants of fractional holdings, and less again for cottagers and altogether landless men;[1] but they did regulate carefully such matters as the length of the '*robot* day' and forbid demands not justified by the law such as 'long haulages', and such oppressive practices as that of taking out all labour days at harvest time, so that the peasant had no time to get in his own crops.

[1] The figure of 156 had been that customary in all the Bohemian Provinces (to which Galicia was then assimilated) and in Styria, Carinthia and Carniola. In Lower Austria it was 104 and in Upper Austria, where the peasants had secured themselves exceptionally favourable terms in the XVIth century, only 14. In Hungary and Croatia it was 52.

Since it was these abuses and illegalities which did constitute the real hardship—the actual obligation of the *robot* was not so burdensome as it sounds[1]—the Patents, where they could be enforced, brought the peasants much real benefit, and it is probable that their condition in some parts of the Monarchy was now well above that of the general Continental level. Maria Theresa met with such stubborn resistance over them from the landlords, especially in Bohemia,[2] that at one moment she thought of cutting the Gordian knot by abolishing the *nexus subditelae* altogether in the Bohemian Provinces (she seems to have thought this unnecessary in the German Provinces, and impracticable in Hungary, after her defeat by the Diet), but the opposition, not only of the Estates, but also of the entire State Council, and of Joseph, forced her to renounce the idea, although most reluctantly—it was one of the occasions on which she thought of abdicating—and content herself with the *Robot* Patent. She did go further on some estates which were at her free disposal, Crown properties, including the lands confiscated from the Jesuits after 1773. On these she introduced a system invented by Hofrat Raab, under which the *dominium utile* of the land was transferred to the peasant holder against a cash rent, so that he became in practice a lease-holder for life. She exhorted private land-

---

[1] 156 days haulage *robot* sounds immense, but this was the figure for a full holding of perhaps 70 acres. If a 'full peasant' had three sons, or employed hired labour, and owned four pairs of oxen or horses, the proportion of his labour which he had to devote to his lord's land even on his *robot* days was only 25 per cent, making 12.5 per cent in the year. A cottager probably did 13 days, the same proportion of his total time.

[2] And not only there; when the consultations were going on, the Styrian landlords had asked for 208 days: the Commissioners wanted 104, and a compromise was eventually reached at the unchanged figure of 156.

lords to imitate this example, but with small results: the traditional system remained the usual one in the Monarchy until 1848.

*   *   *

Educational reform, like other reforms, had come to something of a standstill when the first impetus of van Swieten's changes died away and when the conduct of the war pushed other subjects into the background; the chief *motif* in it thereafter had been the steady eviction of the Jesuits, under relentless pressure from van Swieten, from one stronghold after another. In 1795 a *Studienhof-commission* (Court Commission on Studies) had been established, under the Presidency of the Archbishop of Vienna, at first as an independent body, although later it was incorporated in the United Chancellery, but it had displayed little activity, except for making a few further changes to broaden the curricula of the *gymnasia*.

The big change came only in 1773, when the Society of Jesus was dissolved by the Pope—to the displeasure of Maria Theresa herself, who delayed as long as she could extending the measure to her dominions. The dissolution hardly affected the Universities, from which the Jesuits had by now been excluded almost entirely, but it left an enormous gap in the *gymnasia*, and offered a great opportunity to the 'progressives', who, although van Swieten had died in the preceding year, had by now many representatives on the Commission, including its most prominent member, Count Johann Anton von Pergen, Minister of State and Director of the Oriental Academy.

Von Pergen advocated, firstly, 'complete and permanent supervision by the State of the whole educational system, in all its parts and extent', and secondly, the complete exclusion of the Orders from all instruction, which should be given only by laymen or by 'reliable' secular clergy. Other educationalists wanted such changes made in the curricula of the *gymnasia* as would practically have transformed them into modern schools. It soon became clear that there was no practical possibility of doing without the Orders altogether: there were simply not enough qualified laymen or secular clergy to fill the vacancies, and the radical transformation of the curricula was resisted, not only by Maria Theresa herself, but by many members of the Commission. The Orders were consequently not evicted (and indeed, Maria Theresa allowed many Jesuits to go on teaching), and the *gymnasia* remained *gymnasia*. But the proportion of secular teachers was increased and more modern subjects were introduced into the curricula, while Latin was replaced by modern languages as medium of instruction in many subjects. Further, Maria Theresa herself introduced a number of 'modern' establishments on all levels, from a *Realhandelsakademie* for the training of youths for posts in commerce and industry through schools for apprentices, down to elementary institutions for quite small children.

At this point the question came up whether standards of education should be raised also on the elementary level. The credit for the reform carried through here belongs largely to Maria Theresa herself, for many of her advisers, including von Pergen, held that education was no good thing for the poor, since it only made them conscious of the hardship of their lot, and discontented with it. The view was shared by many, although not all, Churchmen, who thought that education led to Godlessness (not long before, reading had been condemned from the pulpit in Carniola): not to mention that it was heartily endorsed by perhaps the bulk of peasant parents, who did not want to have their children away from the fields, addling their brains with books, still less to pay school fees. But Maria Theresa, whom, on this issue, her son supported strongly, as did Kaunitz, insisted, and even borrowed a famous expert, Felbiger, from Frederick of Prussia. Felbiger produced a blue-print, providing for universal and compulsory elementary education, with a primary (*Trivial*)[1] school in every village, a grammar-school (*Hauptschule*) in every Circle centre and a higher secondary school and a training college (*Normalschule*) in each Provincial capital. The elementary schools were paid for partly by the parents, partly by the manorial lords; the higher schools, by the State, partly out of the revenues from the confiscated property of the Jesuits, which were paid into an 'Educational Fund.' An *Allgemeine Schulordnung* (General Regulations for Schools) embodying these plans was issued for the Western Provinces in 1774.

The goal of universal instruction, even in these Provinces, had naturally not been reached by the time Maria Theresa died, nor, for that matter, until long after, but the advance made even during her life-time was spectacular. Five hundred new schools had been opened, and the numbers of teachers and pupils had risen threefold. 'In no State in the world,' wrote Felbiger, 'is so much care devoted to the lowest schools, as in Austria.'

* * *

The 'progressives' mentioned on the previous page by now constituted such an important element both in the higher bureaucracy of the Monarchy, and among its 'intellectuals,' that even a sketch so short as this must devote some lines to them. It is characteristic of Austrian reformism that it began primarily with a campaign against the omnipotence of the Catholic Church, and that this continued for many years to be a large element in it.

---

[1] So called because what was chiefly taught in them, beside religion, was the *trivium*, i.e., the 'three Rs.'.

Thus the thorough-going Conservatives among Austria's later historians count among the earlier 'subversives' such men as van Swieten and Paul Riegger, who taught canonical and other kinds of law at Vienna University— neither of them interested in social problems, and both pious Catholics, but both champions of State supremacy over the Church. An even more important figure, particularly because he was tutor in law to Joseph and Leopold, both of whose minds he influenced strongly, was Karl Martini, a South Tirolean who came to Vienna in 1753 to fill its new chair of Natural Law, and became the inspiration of a party who about 1765 began to call themselves the 'Party of Enlightenment', by contrast with the 'men of darkness' or 'obscurantists' of the other side from their tenet, which not all their recommenda- tions were, indeed, calculated to promote, that 'en- lightenment', being the source of all progress, must be spread as widely as possible among the peoples.

At first sight, Martini's doctrines sound democratic, or even revolutionary, for he taught that the basis of the State was the social contract, that the executive power derived from the people and that the Prince was only their delegate; furthermore, that men were of nature free, that religous convictions could not be imposed, and that no authority could over-rule the law of nature, which was that of reason. In fact, however, these teach- ings were the parents, or first manifestations, of the authoritarian 'Josephinism' which thereafter, up to 1918, was the rival, as well as at times the ally, of the liberal and democratic movements which were the other enemies of the old order. For Martini made his Prince the embodi- ment and executant of the law of nature, or reason, and allowed him unlimited authority to direct the actions of his subjects in accordance with its dictates. It was true that a subject could never carry out orders which were contrary to law, Divine, natural or prescriptive, but even so, he was not entitled to oppose the Prince, or to gainsay him if he denied that he was violating his moral obligation to observe the law of nature. The second inspiration of the 'Enlightenment', that extraordinary personage, the Rabbi's grandson, Josef Sonnenfels, whose books were used for many years as primers in civics, economics and political science, also laid down that the Prince must rule according to natural law, but it was for him to say what constituted it.

Neither Martini, nor Sonnenfels, nor any other of the 'enlightened' spirits, attacked religion as such: Sonnenfels called it 'undoubtedly the first of all methods of preserving good morality', the indispensable complement to government, able to penetrate where the eye and the arm of the executive could not reach, so that the promotion of it must be a prime object of the Prince's care. But his law, being, by definition, that of reason, was the only one which could prevail, and all other authority must give way to it. This applied to the laws of the Church, and also to 'historic rights' of all kinds, so that the Enlightenment provided theoretical justification for despotism in all fields, civil as well as religious.

Presumably under the pressure of the Enlightened Party, and especially of Joseph, Maria Theresa affirmed her control over the Church considerably in this period, particularly in the last years of it, when Joseph's influence was growing. The dissolution of the Order of Jesus was none of her doing, but a lower age limit of 24 was laid down for admission to any Order, the maximum membership of many Houses was laid down, sometimes at a figure which involved a reduction; one was actually forbidden to take in further members. Church property was put under further control, the disciplinary powers of the Church further restricted. In 1776 the 'Gallican' version of Canonical Law was declared official for the Monarchy.

Even the disabilities under which non-Catholics suffered were lightened a little. In 1778 Protestants were at last allowed to graduate at Vienna University. It became easier for a Protestant to obtain a special exemption to practise some calling (although Maria Theresa had, even before, never boggled at granting such exemptions where she saw profit in it).

This, however, was more indicative of the gradual weakening of her resistance to pressure, than of any change in her convictions. She continued to regard 'general toleration' in her dominions as wrong in principle and detrimental in practice. To the last, her hand pressed so heavily on the Hungarian Protestants that they described her reign as 'the Babylonian Captivity'. As late as 1777 she rejected with drastic words a request from the Supreme Chancellor of Vienna for permission for a family of Jews to settle in Vienna. 'In future,' she wrote, 'no Jews, as they are called, are to be allowed in Vienna without My special permission. I know no worse public plague than this people, with their swindling, usury and money-making, bringing folk to beggary, practising all evil transactions which an honest man abhors: they are therefore to be kept away from here and avoided as far as possible.'

Unmasked crypto-Protestants in Upper Austria, Styria and Carinthia were still being forced to emigrate to Transylvania, or to leave the territory of the Monarchy altogether. A famous case occurred in 1777, when the populations of several Districts in Moravia suddenly revealed Hussite tendencies and refused to attend Catholic Divine Services. She herself hesitated to compel so many thousands of human beings to emigrate, but she did order that all adult male heretics should be pressed into the army or set to forced labour and the women and children imprisoned, and those who continued obdurate, expelled to Hungary. She was eventually persuaded to postpone enforcing the most extreme measures, but only after a most violent clash with her son. The correspondence which passed between the two (Joseph was on his travels when the trouble broke out) is extraordinarily interesting. When Joseph rashly lifted his voice in favour of toleration, she declared roundly that this would be 'the greatest misfortune that would ever have descended on the Monarchy. . . . No dominant religion? Toleration, indifference, are the true means of undermining everything, taking away every foundation. . . . He is no "friend of humanity" who allows everyone his own thoughts.' She ends with a commination service against 'the wicked books whose authors parade their cleverness at the expense of all that is most holy and most worthy of respect in the world, who want to introduce an imaginary freedom which can never exist, and which degenerates into licence and complete revolution.'

She still maintained her hostility to abstract learning, vetoing a second time a proposal to establish an Academy of Sciences, as calculated to open the door to Godlessness and anti-clerical influences. The censorship was actually tightened up in these last years. According to an English visitor (who may, indeed, have been somewhat prejudiced), 'it was hardly credible how many books and publications of every species, and in every language, were proscribed. . . . A sentence reflecting on the Catholic religion, a doubt thrown on the sanctity of some hermit or monk of the Middle Ages, any composition in which the pleasures of love were warmly depicted' was enough to get a book on the index.[1] It goes without saying that the purpose of her educational reform, even although it did involve some extension of laicisation, was not to 'enlighten' the people in any general sense, but simply to

---

[1] N. W. Wraxall, *Memories of the Courts of Berlin, Dresden, Warsaw and Vienna* (Dublin, 1799), vol. II p. 238.

improve their efficiency. It was meant also to promote a special purpose, to which we shall return.

* * *

It may also be mentioned here that Maria Theresa's interest in the arts and in general 'culture' if anything declined during her last years. She had never cared much for these things. If she had Schönbrunn Palace completed on a grand scale (although far less grand than that originally planned, fifty years earlier) and its interior decorated sumptuously, this was rather because she thought the magnificence due to the position of her dynasty than out of artistic pleasure in the effect. It was her husband who was chiefly responsible for the lay-out of the grounds and the enlargement of the zoological and botanical gardens, as he was for the collection of specimens which formed the nucleus of Vienna's later Natural History Museum. She still attended the ballet and opera, but she had never been more musical than the average, by Viennese standards, and never any enthusiastic patron of the arts: artists, musicians and scholars figure only very rarely among the recipients of the benefactions with which she was so generous towards the poor and sometimes so over-lavish towards her immediate public servants.

This was partly due to moral considerations. Without going quite so far as Frederick William of Prussia, who adjured his successor 'not to allow in his lands any comedies, operas, ballets, masques or redoutes, because they are godless and devilish things, whereby Satan and his kingdom are increased', she warned her sons in Italy against 'the bagatelles and *fadeurs* of the theatre', and against gossiping about the actors. 'It is a waste of time to fill one's head with such stuff, it only makes one unfit for sensible conversation.' Actors were 'an evil brood, the most depraved thing in the Monarchy', and she cautioned

Ferdinand, in Milan, against taking the young Mozart into his service. Such men were 'unprofitable'; he should never give them Court posts, for that 'degraded the service.'

When, therefore, on grounds of economy, she cut the expenditure on the Court orchestra and renounced the extravagant performances in which her father had taken pleasure, this cost her no pangs. It was fortunate for the arts that the great magnates of the day, such as the Esterházys, the Nostitzes and the Liechtensteins, patronised them generously in the little Courts which tradition required of them to keep up.

* * *

The prevailing cultural modes of the day, such as they were, were still largely those of Maria Theresa's own youth. Such influences of awakening German national spirit as were seeping across the frontier, were still confined to the 'common people'. The wistful rococo which, towards the end of her reign, was replacing the somewhat over-blown baroque of its beginnings, had nothing Nordic about it. The better-known architects of the day, although many of them now were German-born, had learnt from Italian masters, and built in the Italianate style. The polite language of society was French. Music was Italian or Italianate. Gluck, although he spent many years in Vienna, and although Maria Theresa liked his *Iphigenie* and, exceptionally, gave him a present and a salaried position as Court musician, could not change the tradition, and even his libretti were written by Metastasio, who, having come to Vienna as Court poet in 1730, lived on there for fifty years as arbiter of the elegances. Bach, as a Protestant, found no favour. The theatre attended by society was Italian or French; the broad *Hanswurst* comedies played in the suburbs were for the vulgar (although Francis had enjoyed them).

This was entirely to Maria Theresa's own taste. 'For the theatre,' she wrote, 'I admit that I prefer the least Italian to all our composers, Gaismann, Salieri, Gluck and the rest. Here and there they can make an occasional good piece, but for the ensemble, I always prefer the Italians. In instrumentalisation there is here a certain Haydn who has peculiar ideas, but he is only a beginner.'

* * *

There is space to mention here only two or three of the other fields in which considerable changes were effected. The Commission charged with the revision of the civil law completed a first draft of its work in 1766, but Maria Theresa had it withdrawn for reconsideration: her ruling was that it must be short and lucid, and based as far as possible not on Roman law, but on a natural equity. The pundits were still arguing over it when she died, and it took another generation to give it definitive shape.

A codification of the criminal law, the so-called *Nemesis Theresiana*, was actually sanctioned by her in 1768, but withdrawn owing to the objections of Kaunitz to the publication of a book bearing her name and containing illustrations of torture. The re-issue was then long delayed through the strong advocacy of a party headed by Sonnenfels of the abolition of torture and of the aggravated death penalty, which in the *Nemesis* could take the form of burning alive, impaling, or breaking on the wheel, preceded by preliminary torments. It was precisely Maria Theresa's insistence on retaining both these deterrents that held the work up, although even Joseph was against her and opposed even the death penalty as such, not on humanitarian grounds, but because a living convict could be made to work, and the sight of him perpetuated the memory of the punishment, whereas a dead man was out of mind. It was not until

1776 that Maria Theresa consented to the abolition of torture, and in this field, too, the work was still incomplete when she died.

* * *

The military reforms, which were chiefly the work of Joseph, or more truly, of the relatively young and very capable Lacy, who was made President of the War Council on Daun's death, were for the most part too technical to be described here; but it is impossible to omit mention of the important introduction of a regular system of conscription. In 1771 all the Provinces to which the Haugwitz reforms had applied, except the Tirol (which was allowed to retain its old obligation of general service in case of emergency), were divided into 37 'recruiting areas',[1] each of which had to supply a fixed number of recruits, drawn, in theory, by lot from among those categories of the population which were not legally exempted: chiefly, that is, since almost all other categories were exempted, from the urban and (above all) the rural proletariats. The recruiting was carried out by the army itself: 'the Estates,' Maria Theresa wrote, when appeal was made to her, 'have no voice in the matter.' In practice, lots were seldom drawn: the quotas were brought in by press gangs, who took their victims where they found them.

* * *

Finally, a gradual and tentative restoration was achieved of the public finances. On Francis' sudden death in 1765, a new fall in the State papers had been expected, but things turned out differently. Under Francis' will, made in 1751, Joseph had been left heir to the bulk of his father's personal fortune, amounting, in

[1] The system was extended to Galicia in 1774.

cash, State papers, etc., to some 22 million gulden.
Joseph determined to present all this to the State (thereby
involving himself in an acrid dispute with his brother
Leopold, because there were another 2 million gulden in
Florence, which Joseph demanded and Leopold refused
to give up). The public incineration of the redeemed
papers brought confidence back with such a bound that it
proved possible to reduce the interest on the outstand-
ing debt again, to 4 per cent. The capital of the debt
continued, indeed, to rise—by the end of Maria Theresa's
reign it was 376 million gulden, but meanwhile revenue
receipts were rising also; the budget for 1775 actually
showed a surplus—one of the three recorded in Austrian
history. It is true that things turned for the worse again
in 1779.

* * *

A feature common to so many of the innovations of Maria
Theresa's reign in her Western Provinces that it would be
misleading to link it with any one of them, especially
since it was usually rather consequential and incidental,
than central, and yet one of extreme importance in its
sum effects, was the large measure of Germanisation
introduced under them. Previously, German had indeed
been the language of the central Ministries and of the
higher instances in the German Provinces, and in
practice, of the Bohemian (although there, Czech enjoyed a titular equality with it), but on the manorial
level, business had been transacted, as a matter of course,
in the language understood by the local populations. But
by the end of the 1770s, although no general laws had
been enacted on the subject, it had become customary
and even obligatory on junior officials to report to their
superiors only in German, and if it was necessary to forward a document in another language, to attach a
German translation.

At the same time, the educational system was largely Germanised. Earlier, if any language except Latin was used in teaching, it was that which the pupils would understand. This was, indeed, usually assumed to be German in the Universities, but early in her reign, Maria Theresa rebuked the Jesuits in Prague for not giving enough instruction in Czech, and the teaching in the primary schools, such as they were, was in the local language; it is true that this was given by the authorities, after an enquiry, as the reason for the total absence of any primary schools whatever in the Slovene areas of Styria, since if a Slovene peasant sent his son to school at all, it was only so that he should learn German, and for that, he arranged for him to attend a German school. But as early as 1765 Maria Theresa had ordered that 'attention be paid (in Bohemia) to the further extension of the German language.' In 1770 the instruction was repeated, and 'after three years Latin should no longer be taught in Czech, but in German, and no schoolmaster appointed who did not know German.' The 'General Regulations' of 1774 made German an obligatory subject in all elementary schools in Bohemia. Only the *gymnasia* were allowed to use Czech, for another three years. In the Southern Slav Provinces, including the Military Frontier, to which the system was extended, all secondary education was to be in German. In the primary schools children were to learn their catechism in their mother language at first, but even this concession was to be withdrawn 'gradually, as the German language makes headway.'

A West European writer might spend 100 pages on analysing the philosophy behind this policy, and then the essential truth would probably slip through his words. It was, as German writers, who usually try to have it both ways, rightly maintain, not prompted by any chauvinistic nationalism of the modern type. True, as many of them also record with satisfaction (and the record has its place in a biography of her), she felt herself, personally, a German, and proud of it. We find her writing to her daughter Caroline in Naples 'never to forget that you were born a German, and to take pains to preserve their good qualities, goodness of heart and integrity. . . . Always remain a German at heart in your uprightness, and profess yourself a Neapolitan in all matters which are indifferent, but in none which are evil.' She has reproaches for Marie Antoinette for allowing the French to decry her nation in front of her. 'Do not be ashamed of being a German.'

Certainly, too, she thought of the Empire as a German political formation, gloried in seeing first her husband, then her son, the head of it, took pride as a German in its greatness and regarded her own State primarily as the leading one in that formation. But she was not a Hitler, to despise non-Germans and reject assimilation (which would have shattered her Monarchy within a week) nor a Treitschke, to insist on forcible assimilation in the interests of *Deutschtum*. She would not even have thought this necessary, for there were plenty of precedents for a Province with a non-German population belonging to the Empire. For that matter, the Czech-minded nobles in Bohemia had, at the time, no objections to the connection, while the peasants probably did not know of its existence, and if they had, no one would have thought that their feelings counted.

She had not even anything against the non-Germanic cultures of the Czechs and Slovenes as such: in 1774, the year of the General Regulations, she founded a chair of Czech language at Vienna University. But she wanted an efficient machine. For efficiency, it had to be centralised, and an efficient centralised machine could work smoothly and expeditiously only if it employed a single language, and given the situation as it stood, that language could only be German (granted, too, that this was also more to her taste), most certainly now that it was operating so largely through the medium of writing (that the system exaggerated the necessity of this by its over-insistence on each office controlling the work of those below it, is another point). So the bureaucracy had to be German, and the schools had to be German too, in order to produce the officials, and also to enable the 'subjects' to understand their duties. The reasoning behind the whole system is put with admirable lucidity in the instructions for the schools in the Military Frontier. Instruction in German was necessary to enable the boys to qualify to become officers and N.C.Os. 'without losing their time over the less necessary instruction in Illyrian.' To keep up 'Illyrian' schools as well as German was 'an unjustified burden, oppressive to the military communes.' It does not seem ever to have occurred to Maria Theresa, or to her advisers, that any Czech, Slovene or Croat could find these measures in any way objectionable; nor did they. The administration had not yet acquired the degree of nosiness which it reached in Joseph's time, and enough allowance to avoid oppression was still made for local languages. As for the aspiring Czech and Slovene peasants' sons, they wanted nothing better than to qualify to rise in the world. Precisely because the pace was not overforced, the Germanisation of Bohemia, in particular, made astonishing advances in Maria Theresa's reign.

Maria Theresa did not attempt to Germanise Hungary, the Netherlands or her Italian possessions, which she accepted to be different nationally, as they were historically. She had reconciled herself to leaving the institutions of the two first-named areas intact, which meant that the administration of them could not be Germanised, and it followed that there was no need to Germanise the schools there. Her regime in the Lombardese was autocratic enough, but she was content to leave it, below the top level, in local hands and to conduct it in the local language. She did hope that time would bring a change in Hungary, and indeed, her own Hungarian Chancellery, when preparing a *Ratio Educationis* for the country (they had persuaded her that a separate measure was necessary), wanted German taught in all elementary schools there, and expressed the hope that German would gradually develop, 'as the Court had long wished,' into 'the national language' of Hungary. But she forbore from forcing the pace: it was reserved for her son to do so and by his impetuosity to precipitate the reaction which destroyed for ever the hope of peaceful assimilation.

For the rest, if Joseph's dogmatic impatience accelerated the failure of his mother's hopes, it cannot fairly be said to have caused it. For the paradox is that the very measures introduced to Germanise the Western Provinces, and then unresented there, sowed the seeds of the later Czech and Slovene national revivals which did resent them as unnatural and oppressive. The new schools taught the rising generations to think in German; but they also taught them to think, and in those days, once people began to think, they inevitably came, sooner or later, to think nationally. Consequently, while Maria Theresa's reign produced a Germanisation of the Western Provinces far more extensive than any before it, it also saw (one will not say 'produced', for the true creative agent was the genius of the age) the beginnings of the opposite process.

The whole problem became, of course, much more difficult still when Galicia was annexed in 1773. Here Maria Theresa personally was in favour of complete Germanisation of the administrative and judicial systems, but some of her advisers were uncertain whether Germanisation of the schools would be practicable, or politically prudent, and in the event, only half-measures were taken in the field.

How far any real hope of ever effectively Germanising even the Western Provinces had been strangled at birth by the loss of Silesia is a question on which we can only speculate.

IV

The first of the two major international crises of Maria Theresa's later years—that which ended in the so-called First Partition (more truly, truncation) of Poland—falls within the same period of high activity in which she was busiest with the settlement of her children, and with her second great series of internal reforms. It had begun, in so far as a Polish political crisis can ever be said to have a beginning, as far back as October 7, 1763, with the death of Augustus III, King of Poland and Elector of Saxony, followed only two months later by that of his son, the new Elector, leaving only an infant son. Polish opinion revolted against the idea of a long Regency for another foreign king, and Catherine of Russia seized the opportunity, having bought the consent of Frederick of Prussia with a 12 years' alliance, to impose her own candidate (and ex-lover), Stanislas Poniatowski, who was duly crowned on November 25, 1764.

Maria Theresa would far have preferred, if she could not link Poland to her own system, to see it genuinely independent, rather than a disguised extension of Russia, but she had neither the will nor, at the time, the financial and military resources to challenge the Czarina's move, and she concentrated at first on making the best terms possible for Austria's recognition of the new king. In fact, she was in a fair way to establishing a tolerable relationship with Poniatowski, who proved himself a less docile satellite than Catherine had calculated, when the actions of others carried developments out of her control. The Czarina insisted on political concessions so far-reaching that a party of Poles, banded in the 'Confederation of Bar', revolted, with the result that the Czarina sent troops into Southern Poland: at the same time the Cossacks of the Ukraine rose against their Polish masters. Thereupon, on October 6, 1766, Turkey, alarmed at the extension of Russia's control over the approaches to her territory, declared war on her, with results which were disastrous for herself, for when the 1767 campaign opened, the Russians drove the Turks out of the Danubian Provinces, in which they set up civilian administrations.

The immediate sequel was to draw Austria and Prussia a step nearer to each other, for Frederick, his alliance with Catherine notwithstanding, was no more anxious than Austria to see Russia extend her power too far. There had been a suggestion before that Frederick and Joseph might meet, but Maria Theresa had not liked the idea. Now she withdrew her objections, and the two men met at Neisse in August, 1769. The meeting went off politely enough, but it produced no solution for the Polish question, neither did a second meeting (this time attended by Kaunitz) in September, 1770, at Mährisch-Neustadt. The Porte had asked both Austria and Prussia for their mediation, which, as things stood, would have meant putting pressure on Russia to withdraw. Frederick felt his hands tied by his alliance, while Maria Theresa was not prepared to undertake the thankless and possibly even dangerous role. Polite generalities were exchanged, but the Polish question was hardly even mentioned.

But by now the idea of partition was ripening in Frederick's mind. From his youth up, he had cherished the ambition of annexing West Prussia, and in the autumn of 1769 had made a tentative suggestion to the effect in St.

Petersburg. This had, indeed, been coldly received at the time, and in 1770, when the Austrian Minister in Berlin (apparently acting without instructions) dropped a hint that Frederick might re-cede Silesia, compensating himself in Poland, Frederick was in one of his timorous moods and did not dare to re-open the question.

But in the autumn of 1770 Catherine began to find the combination of Turkish armies and Polish insurgents to be, after all, a strain on her strength. Nervous of Austria's reactions if she pressed for annexation of the Danubian Provinces, she thought expansion in Poland the safer course. She remembered Frederick's suggestion, with less disinclination than before. Meanwhile, Austria had been led into what proved to be an indiscretion. In February, 1769, Poniatowski had himself asked the Austrian troops, which had been placed along the frontier in a precautionary cordon, to occupy the district of Szepes (Zips), in which some of his opponents had taken refuge. The Szepes, however, was technically Hungarian territory, for although it had been pledged to Poland in 1412 and had ever since remained under Polish administration, it had never been formally ceded. When the request was granted, which was done in order to avoid taking sides with what were technical rebels, Kaunitz had the order given in virtue of Maria Theresa's sovereign rights over the territory. He adopted this form to avoid prejudicing technical rights, but he punctiliously assured all foreign Missions in Vienna that Austria had no intention of infringing Poland's occupational rights, and in fact, none of them raised any objections. But someone then dug up some old documents purporting to show that the early frontier had run some distance north of the area usually recognised as that of the Szepes. In July, 1770, the Austrian cordon advanced to the line claimed, and the official sent to take charge of the occupied territory gave himself the title of 'Administrator of the Re-incorporated Province'. When the Polish Chancellor protested, Kaunitz answered maintaining Hungary's legal right to the territory, although expressing the wish to reach an amicable settlement.

The validity of the titles themselves seems to have been somewhat dubious, and the move (which was probably made on Joseph's initiative) was certainly a foolish one. Catherine seized her chance, and in January, 1771, sent Frederick word that since Austria had set the example, she did not see why other Powers should not follow it. Frederick took the suggestion up with enthusiasm: the question, he replied, 'was no longer one of maintaining Poland intact, since the Austrians wanted to truncate it', but of preventing the dismemberment from upsetting the balance of power.

The further diplomatic history of the question was now simply that of haggling over who should get what. It was immensely complicated, because it was not only Polish territory over which the three Courts bargained, but also Turkish, and in respect of Turkey, Austria had tied her hands, for in the spring of 1771 Kaunitz and Joseph had, strongly against Maria Theresa's judgement, but overriding her objections—this was one of the cases when she let herself be overruled—initiated conversations with the Porte, and, on July 6/7, a secret convention had been concluded, under which Austria promised to use her influence to secure Turkey acceptable peace terms, if possible on the basis of the *status quo ante bellum*, in return for the cession of Little Wallachia (west of the Olt) and cash subsidies. The first of these had, although the convention had not yet been ratified, been paid on the nail.

The details of the negotiations do not belong in a sketch such as this of Maria Theresa's life. Since Kaunitz and Joseph, to whom she left them, put forward demands which left Frederick astounded at 'the size of Austria's appetite', and since, when the Treaty of Partition was signed on July 25/August 2, 1772, Austria actually got substantially the largest share of the three, in area and population (all Galicia, with 2,600,000 inhabitants, not counting the Bukovina, to which Joseph helped himself three years later as prize for 'mediating' peace between Russia and the Porte, against Russia's 1,600 from Poland, and Prussia's 600,000),[1] and Maria Theresa ended by accepting this with no more resistance than that she boggled at the adjective from the phrase 'just claims' in the manifesto in which the annexation had been announced to the Poles—in view of this, it is possible to understand the sarcasms levelled at her. 'Elle pleure mais elle prend,' wrote Frederick, and the French Ambassador in Vienna had the same picture: 'she carved territory out of Poland with one hand, and used her handkerchief with the other.' But the easy quips were unjust. She would genuinely have preferred the *status quo*. When she saw that this could not possibly be preserved, she tried to get Frederick to compensate her in Silesia, which she really felt to be a just claim. When Frederick would not hear of this, she flatly rejected as dishonourable, in view of the secret treaty (even although she had disapproved of it), alternative suggestions that Austria might compensate herself in the Balkans at the expense of the Porte (Kaunitz did not care for that idea, either). In the end, it was Poland or nothing, and it would have been humanly, and practically, impossible for her to sit back while Prussia and Russia tilted the balance dangerously against Austria. But her scruples had been perfectly sincere, and her political judgement on the whole transaction was sound. '*Placet*,' she wrote in the

---

[1] The comparison gives, of course, an unfair position of the real gains, for it does not count the very large acquisitions made by Russia at the expense of Turkey.

end, when signing the manifesto, 'because so many great and learned men want it. But when I am long dead, people will see what is the outcome of this violation of every accepted standard of sanctity and justice.' She told Joseph that the Partition had cost her ten years of life; it was the source of all ill which would descend on the Monarchy, and would end by destroying it.

Historians have often quoted the famous memorandum written by her to Kaunitz after Frederick had refused to surrender any Silesian territory. 'The easiest course,' she wrote, 'would certainly be to accept the offer made to us of participating in the partition of Poland. But where is the justice in robbing an innocent party which we have always prided ourselves on defending and supporting? To what purpose are all these vast and costly preparations, all these loud, threatening affirmations of our determination to preserve the balance in northern Europe? The single motive of interest that we should not remain alone between the two other Powers without securing an advantage does not seem to me a sufficient, or even an honourable, pretext for joining in with two unjust usurpers with the purpose of thrusting a third still further down, without any legal title.

'I do not understand a policy which, when two use their superior strength to oppress an innocent victim, allows and enjoins a third to imitate them and to commit the same injustice, as a simple precaution for the future, and out of present expediency: this seems to me untenable. A Prince has no more rights than any other mortal; the greatness and support of his State will not avail him when the day comes when we must all give account for our actions . . .'

And of the suggestion that Austria should compensate herself at the expense of the Porte:

'I will even go so far as to say that to do no man injustice is not an act of magnanimity, but an effect of true principles. We have allied ourselves with the Porte, we have even accepted money from it; to find pretexts to make the Turks take a first false step and then enrich ourselves at their expense is in no way consonant with scrupulous honesty and true principles. I would never consent to it. . . .'

She was, it may be remarked, almost as displeased over Joseph's pouching of the Bukovina. She acquiesced in this, too, but she wrote to Mercy that Austria was 'completely in the wrong. . . . I admit, I do not know how we shall get out of this—hardly with honour, and that grieves me quite inexpressibly.'

Her letter to Kaunitz contains another remarkable and characteristic passage. Since honour precluded the acquisition of Serbia and Bosnia, 'the only Provinces which would bring us advantage, we are left with Wallachia and Moldavia' (she seems to have regarded these as already lost to the Porte), 'unsalubrious, devastated countries, exposed to the Turks, Tatars and Russians, with no fortresses, lands on which we should have to spend many millions of money and many men to retain hold of them. Our Monarchy can do without an enrichment of this kind, which would end by ruining it altogether.'

The temptation is irresistible to cap these quotations with a still more drastic appreciation from her pen of the Balkans and their inhabitants; particularly since the lines also testify to her sound outlook on Austria's real interest in the 'Eastern Question'. It comes from a letter written by her to Mercy, in July 1777, when Joseph was again toying with expansionist thoughts.

'The partition of the Ottoman Empire,' she wrote, 'would be, of all enterprises, the most reckless and dangerous. What should we gain, if we were to extend our conquests to the walls of Constantinople itself? Unsalubrious, uncultivated provinces, inhabited either not at all, or by unreliable Greeks,[1] which would not add to the forces of the Monarchy, but rather exhaust them. This would be an event even more critical than the Partition of Poland . . . I will never lend my hand to a partition of the Porte, and I hope that my grandchildren after me will see the Turks in Europe.'

It was unfortunate indeed for Austria that Joseph shared neither his mother's continence, nor her sane outlook on the Eastern Question. Hardly were her eyes closed when he joined hands with Catherine of Russia in that fatal enterprise in the Balkans which was the immediate cause of the ruin of all his hopes, and of his own death.

V

The Polish crisis had not broken the continuity of Maria Theresa's work in the domestic field: it is not possible to differentiate between the nature of those which ante-date the Partition and those—which include some of the most important—which reached maturity after it. This is our justification for not dividing our account of them. In her, however, a change was now very perceptible. Whether or no the crisis took ten years off her life, she was an old woman by the end of it, and a sad and lonely one. The departure into the world of nearly all her children had left her very much alone, for she had never had many intimates outside her family circle, and nearly all the friends and close confidants of her early days were dead. Countess Fuchs had died in 1755, Koch in 1763, Haugwitz in 1765, Daun in 1766, Bartenstein in 1767, Silva Tarouca in 1771, van Swieten in 1772. Kaunitz, of course, was still there, but of the newer men there were only a handful—Mercy, Lacy, and perhaps one or two more—to whom she opened her heart as she had to

[1] i.e., members of the Greek-Orthodox Church.

Kinsky, Khevenhüller and Daun. Physically she was growing inactive as her corpulence gained on her, aggravating the after-effects of her sixteen pregnancies, her attack of small-pox and a nasty accident when she was thrown from a carriage. She now hardly left Vienna, except for periodic visits to 'Mimi' and her husband in near-by Pozsony: it was with difficulty that she was persuaded to visit Prince Esterházy's magnificent new palace of Esterháza, only a few miles further away. She spent as much of her time as she could in Schönbrunn, the rest in Vienna, rarely leaving even the Hofburg except to attend public Divine Service. Much of her time was spent in private devotions.

Nor can it be denied that in her conduct of, and her attitude towards, public affairs, she was not the woman that she was. The files show, indeed, little slackening of her diligence, or of her acumen: many a man thirty years her junior could have envied her either. Also, when she saw something wrong which needed mending, she set about mending it with all her old vigour. But her determination was weaker: it was now not infrequent for her, if she found the opposition to her wishes strong (this happened oftenest when she found Kaunitz and Joseph combining against her) suddenly to throw up the sponge and retire to her devotions, leaving the others to clear up the mess.

More important still, she now saw less and less that needed mending. The Monarchy of the day was, after all, largely her creation, and she was, on the whole, satisfied with what she had made of it. So, too, with her helpers: they were the men of her choice, and she had grown used to them, as they to her. By 1775 the great innovator of 1745 had grown into a conservative.

This was an abiding source of irritation to Joseph, who thought that everything she had done was a mere series of half-measures, resulting in stagnation. 'Everything is in arrears,' he wrote to his brother in 1774; 'nothing is done, people kill themselves for nothing, and affairs go from bad to worse.' We have mentioned some of the occasions of conflict, and can find space only for one more, the second of the two major international crises of the co-Regency. Here Maria Theresa ended (although she did not so begin) by putting her foot down and asserting her will, although only at the cost of an elemental conflict with her son.

The crisis, like that which opened her reign, although with the roles of aggressor and defender reversed, concerned Bavaria, where the death in 1770 of the brother of the Prince Elector had left the Elector Palatine, Karl Theodore, of the cadet branch of the Wittelsbachs, heir apparent to the family dignities and possessions. There were, however, other claimants to many of the titles, among them Prussia, which had an old claim on the Rhineland Duchies of Jülich-Berg. Austria, too, could show documents dating from 1353 entitling the Duke of Austria to the reversion of parts of Lower Bavaria, and other areas were technically fiefs of the Bohemian Crown. It was also possible for Joseph to claim the disposition over all Bavaria as an escheated fief of the Reich. Both Joseph and Kaunitz were anxious for the acquisition, and opened negotiations with Karl Theodore, who was not averse from a deal, on terms, and an agreement had been reached, but not yet signed, under which Karl Theodore acknowledged Austria's titles under the 1353 transaction in return for acknowledgement of his other titles, when, on December 30, 1777, the Elector of Bavaria died, whereupon his Ministers proclaimed Karl Theodore ruler over the whole Electorate.

Joseph at once prepared to send troops into Bavaria, and he had in fact secured legal title for making good some of his claims, for on January 3, 1778, the Elector's plenipotentiary had signed the agreement described above, with the possibility of further negotiated exchanges. Maria Theresa thought the claim flimsy, and was convinced that the attempt to enforce it—still more, to occupy all Bavaria—would lead to dangerous international complications. 'I have,' she wrote, 'never seen an enterprise of the kind succeed, with the single exception of that of 1741 against me, which cost me Silesia. The irruption into Saxony, that in Portugal, ours in 1756 —none of them came off. All ruined those who undertook them. Are we not still feeling the consequences—200 millions more of debts and the prosperity of our peoples ruined?' But he insisted, and she gave way again, and when the luckless Karl Theodore, put in a difficult position by the proclamation in Munich, tarried with the ratification, Joseph threatened him with an Imperial distraint, and ordered his troops to move: they crossed the frontier on January 16. The ratification arrived, and as the Austrian army was not opposed, Joseph flattered himself that his coup had come off. But it was his mother, not he, who had judged the international situation aright. France was icily disapproving, and Frederick determined that Austria should gain no more ground in Germany. Pretending that he was protecting the interests of the next heir presumptive, the Duke of Zweibrücken, he entered a formal protest. Austria and the Palatine began negotiations for a 'settlement', the object of which, as Joseph saw it, was that the Elector Palatine should obtain sufficient compensation elsewhere to allow Austria to annex all Bavaria, but the parties could not agree. As the conversations went on, Frederick contrived to block every suggested composition. Meanwhile, he fomented opposition to Austria in the Empire and assembled a large army on the Bohemian frontier, across which, after Joseph had rejected the last of his proposals, he led it on July 5.

This spurred Maria Theresa to one of the most

desperate throws of her life. During the spring, while the negotiations were going on, she had repeatedly urged her son to make ever larger concessions rather than let things come to a war which, apart from its moral aspects, could, she was convinced, only end in disaster to the Monarchy. Now, after receiving a panicky letter from Joseph, who had quite lost his nerve, she sent a personal emissary to Frederick assuring him of her strong desire for peace and asking for resumption of the interrupted negotiations. She had consulted Kaunitz before taking the step, but Joseph was informed only after the messenger had started.

He, meanwhile, had recovered his nerve, and the news sent him into an extreme of fury. His letters to his mother at this juncture breathe a cold anger which cut her to the quick, although they failed to move her. Humanly, these were probably the bitterest hours of her life, except those after her husband's death. Only her deep conviction that she was doing right sustained her. The irony of it all was that in the end, things turned out quite differently from expectation. Frederick agreed to re-open negotiations, but spun them out in the hope of profiting from the disagreement between mother and son, always raising his price, and meanwhile advancing deeper into Bohemia. But then he was himself outwitted. Joseph, or rather, Lacy and Laudon, outmanoeuvred him, and he withdrew without venturing battle (the war in fact cost no bloodshed at all: it was afterwards nicknamed the 'potato war' or 'plum shindy'). France and Russia intervened to mediate, and after wearisome negotiations, peace was signed at Teschen on Maria Theresa's 62nd birthday, May 13, 1779.

Austria acquired the small accession of the 'Innviertel' between the Danube and the Salzach. For Joseph it was a bitter humiliation, which he tried to avenge four years later, to be frustrated again by Frederick, this time without even mobilisation. For his mother, on the other hand, it was an occasion of profound satisfaction. On May 23 she had a great thanksgiving service for peace held in the Cathedral of St. Stephen. 'Today,' she wrote to Kaunitz, 'I have ended my career gloriously with a Te Deum. With His help I have ended what I joyfully undertook for the tranquillity of my own lands, heavy as its cost was to me; the rest will not amount to much.'

Her life's work was, indeed, about done. The only event of first-class importance in the year which followed was Joseph's visit (of which his mother disapproved strongly, but he disregarded her protests) to Catherine of Russia; and this belongs historically rather to his reign than to hers. She was concerned chiefly with domestic and family affairs; although she also took an active part in the unravelling of the imbroglio created by the Bavarian enterprise. Then, in November 1780, she was attacked by severe bronchial trouble and presently developed a fever. She saw her end nearing and met it with complete fortitude. She was a restless patient, partly because she found it hard to breathe lying down; she spent most of her hours in an arm-chair. She worked on State papers, or on codicils to her will, almost to the very end. Most of her children had by now gathered round her. On the evening of the 29th she struggled up from her chair, took a few steps, and sank on a couch. 'Your Majesty is lying uncomfortably,' said Joseph, who was with her. 'Yes,' she answered, 'but well enough to die.' A few moments later, she was no more. She was buried on December 3. Her remains lie in the family vault of her ancestors, in the crypt of the Capuchin Church of Vienna, beside those of her husband, in the sumptuous sarcophagus made for him and her by the sculptor Balthazar Moll.

* * *

Maria Theresa had her full share of human shortcomings. She was habitually, and often formidably, short of temper, managing, unsentimental, tough: at times she could be surprisingly hard. Her intellect, naturally un-brilliant and not polished by any thorough schooling, could almost be called narrow. Her lack of deep artistic sense was symptomatic of a general unimaginativeness. She was not easily open to new ideas, nor attracted by them. Abstractions and generalisations were not her field at all.

But these were the defects of very great qualities. Her heart, when it was reached, was warm and generous, as quick to forgiveness as it was to wrath. If she saw that she had hurt, she was genuinely distressed, and knew how to make amends with a rare grace and charm. She was loyal, even to excess, towards those who served her faithfully. She was genuinely and deeply God-fearing, unswervingly upright, as scrupulous for the rights of others as she was touchy in the defence of her own, and dauntless of courage. Her hardihood may in her youth have contained a dash of the gambler's spirit, but this was no loss where the spirit of adventure was, in general, so dismally lack-ing as it was in her Court.

If her vision was not wide, it was needle-sharp, and her lack of philosophic outlook was fully compensated by great shrewdness, horse-sense and sanity of judge-ment: this last was, indeed, something of an acquired quality, liable to be clouded by personal considerations, especially where the two great passions of her life were involved, her adoration of her husband and her loathing of Frederick of Prussia. Her diligence was inexhaustible.

If we survey her achievement, we must agree that all the imperfections which Joseph found in it were really present. Every single one of her reforms was in fact in-complete, in one respect or another. The unification and centralisation stopped short at the frontiers of Hungary, to which none of the other reforms, except those relating to the peasants, applied at all, while even in the Western Provinces large gaps remained to be filled. The peasants were still not free men, the educational system still wore the blinkers of the Counter-Reformation, the new bureaucracy was still only half a bureaucracy, the old aristocracy set to perform a new role and doing so with only half a heart. Joseph was, moreover, quite right in his criticisms of its cumbersome and ineffectual working: in some respects the over-centralised machine, with its insufficient delegation of responsibility, probably produced less satisfactory results than the crude and summary methods of the old systems, which at least had operated on a basis of local knowledge.

Many things had been left undone, among them a considerable number which would have been desirable in theory, and perfectly feasible in practice. But if we consider, not only—as he did—what remained to do, but what had been done since 1740, the picture appears in a very different light. There was hardly a field of her subjects' lives which Maria Theresa had left untouched: she had been far the greatest moderniser in the history of her dynasty. She had carried through an immense work, and that without provoking a single serious revolt: on the contrary, the sum effect had been to produce a steady reinforcement of the centripetal forces in every part of the Monarchy, not even excluding Hungary. It is even possible to say that it was only under her hand that the Habsburg Monarchy ceased to be a purely dynastic expression and received something of a corporate soul— perhaps no very deep or universal sense of self-consciousness, but so much that it survived of its own will for a century and a half longer, and when it perished, did so by no means unreluctantly.

If this is so, it was her achievement, and it can even be

said that it was due in large part to the very limitations of her mentality, teaching her as they did to approach each individual problem in a pragmatic and undogmatic spirit, eschewing generalisations or innovations beyond what she saw to be necessary in each particular case. For it is possible to reform too much, as well as too little, and, as Joseph found to his cost, it can be far more dangerous.

For Further Reading

Bibliographies: K. and M. Uhlirz, *Handbuch der Geschichte Oesterreichs und seiner Nachbarländer Böhmen und Ungarn*, 4 vols., Graz, 1927ff (*Vol. I* for foreign relations, *II.I* for domestic); near-exhaustive for works in German up to date of publication; new edition now (1969) in preparation. J. Roach, *Bibliography of Modern History*, Cambridge, 1968. Shorter bibs. in works by Mayr-Kaindl-Pirchegger, Zöllner and Pick (below).

Maria Theresa's own voice is to be heard (apart from her innumerable annotations to State papers) in her letters and her *Political Testaments*. Most of the main series of her letters were edited by her biographer, A. von Arneth: her correspondence with Marie Antoinette, 2 vols., Vienna, 1866; with Joseph (also Joseph's letters to Leopold), 3 vols., Vienna, 1867; her secret correspondence with Mercy, 3 vols., 1874; *Letters to her Children and Friends*, 4 vols., 1881; her letters to Maria Antonia of Saxony, ed. M. Lippert, 1908. Her letters to Joseph and Marie Antoinette are the subject of two studies by G. P. Gooch in his *M.T. and other Studies*, London, 1927.

The *Testaments* were edited (with a much-needed glossary) by J. Kallbrunner, Vienna, 1952; a translation of the first, and longer, in C. A. Macartney, *Evolution of the Habsburg and Hohenzollern Dynasties*, N.Y., 1969.

Documents: foreign relations: see the bibs. For Podewils' reports, *Podewils, Diplomatische Berichte*, ed. Dr. Carl Hinrichs, Berlin, 1937. See also *Die Relationen der Botschafter Venedigs*, ed. Arneth, *Fontes Rerum Austriacarum, II. 22*, Vienna, 1863. Robinson's despatches have never been edited; they are preserved in the P.R.O. as the *Grantham Papers*. Domestic: a 9-vol. collection of all edicts, etc., relating to the Western Provinces was published in Vienna in 1785 as *Sammlung aller für die k. Erbländer ergangenen Gesetze und Verordnungen 1740-1780*. A selection of the central documents is given by E. Fellner and J. Kretschmayer, *Die oesterreiche Zentralverwaltung, Abt. I Bd. 1-3* (text) and *Abt. II* (commentary) (*Archiv für oesterreichische*

Geschichte, vols. 82, 104). Her Hungarian laws: *Magyar Törvény-tár 1760–1835*, Ed. D. Csiky and D. Markus, Budapest, 1901.
Contemporary memoirs, etc.: a generally barren field, except for the enormous diary kept by M.T.'s Lord Marshal, Count J. J. Khevenhüller, edited as *Aus der Zeit M.T.s* by Count Rudolph Khevenhüller-Metsch and H. Schlitter, 7 vols., 1907–25 (intimacies of Court life). Also Karoline Pichler, *Denkwürdigkeiten aus meinem Leben*, ed. E. K. Blümml, 2 vols., Munich, 1914.

Biographies: The classic biography of M.T. is and remains that of Arneth, 10 vols., Vienna, 1863–79. Arneth was for many years Director of the Austrian State archives, and no document reached that repository of which he did not take cognisance. It is true that a question not a subject of documentary discussion simply did not exist for him. The fullest of the later lives is that by E. Guglia, 2 vols., Munich, 1917, good on the internal side. Other later biogs. in German are those by H. Kretschmayer, 2nd ed., Gotha, 1938, by a trained historian; K. Tschuppik, Vienna, 1934, journalistic, much military detail; P. Reinhold, Vienna, 1957, sometimes penetrating, very summary on internal developments. The fullest of the works in English are those by C. L. Morris, London, 1938, and R. Pick, N.Y. and London, 1966, (only up to 1757). See also Gooch, op. cit.. The little biography by M.T. Bright, London, 1897 is mainly diplomatic, and the later years are covered not in this work but in its sequel, *Joseph II*.

Other figures: This is not the place to list the literature on Joseph II, all, incidentally, inadequate except the work of Mitranov. Biogs. of Francis, F. Hennings, *Und sitzet ihr zur linken Hand*, Vienna, 1961; Maria Christina, by A. Wolf, 2 vols., Vienna, 1863; Daun, by F. von Thadden, Vienna, 1968; Silva Tarouca, by F. Silva Tarouca, *Der Mentor der Kaiserin*, Vienna, 1960. Nothing worthy of them has yet been written on Kaunitz or Haugwitz, but good short sketches of them and of some other figures, including Bartenstein and van Swieten, in F. Walter, *Die Männer um M. T.*, Vienna, 1951. For Sonnenfels see A. Kann, *A Study in Austrian Intellectual History*, London, 1960.

Histories: The latest standard histories in German are those of H. Hantsch, *Geschichte Oesterreichs* 3rd ed., 2 vols., Vienna, 1964, (M.T. in vol. II); E. Zöllner, same title, 2nd ed., 1961; Mayr-Kaindl-Pirchegger, 5th ed., 3 vols., Vienna, 1966, (M.T. in vol. II.) The English language has still produced no general account since Coxe's *House of Austria*, 3rd ed., 3 vols., 1873.

Accounts of the diplomatic and military events of the period are conveniently found in the *New Cambridge Modern History*, *Vol. VII*, cc. *xvii–xx* and *Vol. VIII*, cc. *ix–xiii*. For further references see the bibs. above, also the bibs. at the ends of the chapters in the older *C.M.H.* There are some pages on internal developments up to 1763 in the *New C.M.H.*, *VII.* c. *xvii*, and on the later years, id. *VIII.*, c. *x*. It may be mentioned here that so far as internal developments are concerned, the Austrian histories hardly look outside the German-Austrian Provinces; at the most, they throw a side-glance at Bohemia. For Bohemia, the best general work is still that of E. Denis, *La Bohème depuis la Montagne Blanche*, 2 vols., Paris, 1903: shorter, and somewhat disappointing, J. Kerner, *Bohemia in the XVIIIth Century*, N.Y., 1932. For Hungary, little in any language but Magyar, except H. Marczali's *Hungary in the XVIIIth century*, Cambridge, 1910; short, C. A. Macartney, *Hungary, A Short History*, 2nd ed., Edinburgh, 1966. For the Netherlands and Lombardy, see the bibs. A general sketch of how the Monarchy stood (all aspects) in 1780 in C. A. Macartney, *The Habsburg Empire, 1790–1918*, London, 1969. See also W. Andreas, *Das theresianische Oe. während des XVIIIten Jahrhunderts*, Gotha, 1938. An excellent short account of the Haugwitz reforms in F. Walter, *Das theresianische Staatsreform von 1749*, Vienna, 1958. Nothing so good on the later manipulations. The State Council: C. Hock and H. I. Bidermann, *Der. oe. Staatsrat*, Vienna, 1879. Most refreshing and enlightening, for both administrative and cultural questions, Vol. I of I. Beidtel, *Gesch. der oe. Staatsverwaltung*, 2 vols., Innsbruck, 1896, but written ca. 1850. So far nothing definitive on economic developments, but see G. Otruba, *Die Wirtschaftspolitik M.T.s*, Vienna, 1963, with full bib.. The peasant question has so far been dealt with adequately only for the Bohemian Provinces— by K. Grünberg, *Die Bauernbefreiung*, etc., 2 vols., Leipzig,

1893, and for Hungary by I. Acsady and D. Szabó (in Hungarian). Cultural questions: Arneth, Guglia and Kann, op. cit.; also vol. I of J. Maas, *Der Josephinismus*, 4 vols., Vienna, 1950 ff and the bibs.. Nationality (Western Provinces only): A. Fischel, *Oe. Sprachenrecht*, Brünn, 1910, and the section in my *Habsburg Empire* (above).

Index